FIGHTERS
FOR
INDEPENDENCE

Clements Library Bicentennial Studies

This series is made possible by a grant from
Lilly Endowment, Inc.

The Toll of Independence: *Engagements & Battle
Casualties of the American Revolution*,
edited by Howard H. Peckham

The Sinews of Independence: *Monthly Strength
Reports of the Continental Army*, edited by Charles H. Lesser

*Fighters for Independence: A Guide to
Sources of Biographical Information on
Soldiers and Sailors of the American
Revolution*, edited by J. Todd White and Charles H. Lesser

FIGHTERS
FOR
INDEPENDENCE

*A Guide to Sources
of Biographical Information
on Soldiers and Sailors
of the American Revolution*

Edited by

J. TODD WHITE *and* CHARLES H. LESSER

THE UNIVERSITY OF CHICAGO PRESS

Chicago   *London*

J. TODD WHITE has been a research associate at the William L. Clements Library and a visiting research fellow at the U.S. Army Center of Military History.

CHARLES H. LESSER is assistant director for archives and publications at the Department of Archives and History of the state of South Carolina. He served as research editor of the American Revolution Bicentennial Project, William L. Clements Library, and edited *The Sinews of Independence: Monthly Strength Reports of the Continental Army.*

THE UNIVERSITY OF CHICAGO PRESS, CHICAGO 60637
THE UNIVERSITY OF CHICAGO PRESS, LTD., LONDON

© 1977 by The University of Chicago
All rights reserved. Published 1977
Printed in the United States of America

81 80 79 78 77   9 8 7 6 5 4 3 2 1

Library of Congress Cataloging in Publication Data
White, J.   Todd.
  Fighters for independence.

  (Clements Library bicentennial studies)
  Includes index.
  1.   United States—History—Revolution, 1775-1783—
Biography—Bibliography—Union lists.   2.   United States—
History—Revolution, 1775-1783—Sources—Bibliography—
Union lists.   3.   United States—Genealogy—Bibliography—
Union lists.   4.   Catalogs, Union—United States.
  I.   Lesser, Charles H.   II.   Title.   III.   Series.
Z1238.W45   [E206]   016.9733'092'2   [B]   77-78068
ISBN 0-226-89498-3

CONTENTS

☆

FOREWORD

☆

This volume is primarily a service work for historical researchers and genealogists. It tells nothing about the American Revolution itself, but where to find information on the men who bore arms — soldiers, sailors, and marines. It incidentally indicates the enormous number and variety of personal records which survive from that war. The orderly delineation of them and their locations cuts a path through the thickly forested wilderness of military paper work.

Experienced ancestor-hunters have been aware of some of these clusters of records but rarely of all of them. Professional historians have also known about certain classes of documents, but seldom about the full panoply of manuscript and printed sources available on military participants.

This bibliography began to develop out of other researches undertaken at this library for the current Studies series. Further investigation was then pursued to cover certain new areas of source material. We hope the guide proves helpful.

Howard H. Peckham, Director
William L. Clements Library
University of Michigan

INTRODUCTION

☆

For many decades the historian and the genealogist have moved along parallel paths. Within the last several years, however, their respective fields have been converging.[1] The historian's interest in family history and the social and spatial mobility of population has taken him into groups of records, such as marriage and birth registers, which have traditionally been within the purview of the genealogist. At the same time there has been an increasing sophistication in genealogical research. This guide is intended to serve the needs of both groups.

The military participants of the American Revolution are unique among nonelite groups in the extent to which their lives have been recorded. One result of the revolutionary war was the proliferation of a vast body of records pertaining to the administration of the military forces. Muster and pay rolls, descriptive lists of soldiers, and petitions for promotion or permission to resign document the military service record of many thousands of individuals. Detailed documentation did not cease when the armies and navies were disbanded. Postwar claims for back pay, bounty land records, and most important, applications for revolutionary war pensions continued to record the lives of these men — and through them, their families — well into the nineteenth century. Because a significant portion of the revolutionary generation is traceable from young adulthood through old age, exciting possibilities exist for historical research.

These resources are all the more attractive since they are easy to exploit. The biographical information in these records has long appealed to genealogists in their search for revolutionary ancestors. In direct response to the interests of the genealogical community, especially members of the patriotic societies, the custodians of military and pension records have done much to make them available and to facilitate their use. The records of Connecticut have been published.

1. For an interesting and important article on this subject, see Samuel P. Hays, "History and Genealogy: Patterns of Change and Prospects for Cooperation," *Prologue: The Journal of the National Archives* 7 (1975):39-43, 81-84, 187-91.

New Jersey and North Carolina have compiled and published lists of soldiers and sailors from state records, and Massachusetts has published seventeen volumes of military service records compiled from the state's archival holdings. Unpublished manuscript collections have been organized, indexed, and microfilmed. All of this work, and more, exists to aid those who are interested in pursuing historical and genealogical research through military records.

The first chapter of this Guide covers military and related records that contain biographical information on the military participants of the American Revolution. The text discusses such records as revolutionary war rolls, orderly books, and types of documents found in legislative records and collected papers of high-ranking officers. Reference is made to compiled service records and finding aids, and the value and limitations of the revolutionary war pension application files are indicated. Accompanying the text is a list of microfilmed collections in the National Archives, published collections of revolutionary war rolls, and published records relating to the administration of revolutionary war pensions.

The second chapter is an annotated bibliography of published and unpublished lists of soldiers and sailors, which contain varying amounts of biographical information. For the most part, the lists are based on the types of documentary evidence discussed in chapter 1. They range widely in scope, but the majority of them have been compiled by the genealogical community or for their use. The value of these works is that they save both the historian and the genealogist much time and effort researching documents for information that has already been collected. Indeed, the availability of these collected data may suggest avenues for research.

Types of works listed in this second chapter are compiled service records; lists of soldiers for various states, military units, and branches of the service; pension application abstracts; and biographical sketches of officers and men. Some of the more interesting items have been compiled by members of the Daughters of the American Revolution. Their dedication in preserving the record and memory of all soldiers and sailors, not just their own ancestors, has resulted in a highly valuable body of works through which patterns of westward migration may be studied. Among these are works dealing with soldiers who moved to the new states of Ohio, Indiana, Illinois, and Missouri. The applicability of such research to demographic history is immediately apparent.

The third chapter directs researchers to additional sources of information. A complete bibliography of materials pertinent to biographical research on revolutionary war soldiers was impossible. Genealogical libraries and local historical societies hold typescript compilations of servicemen which may be found nowhere else. The hundreds of local histories published during the nineteenth and early twentieth centuries often contain lists of soldiers. Muster and pay rolls, lists of soldiers, and similar data may also be found in the publications of state historical societies and genealogical societies. Included in this chapter are lists of published guides to manuscript collections, bibliographies of state and local history, and guides to genealogical research.

The fourth chapter is a bibliography of diaries, journals, memoirs, and autobiographies of military participants. This traditional source of historical interpretation not only contains biographical and genealogical material, but also permits a view of the war and American society which can be found in no other records. There are approximately five hundred separate items, many with multiple references, in this final section.

Following chapter 4 is a major-subject index providing access to works cited which deal with specific states and subjects, such as prisoners and westward migration.

This guide is the result of the successive work of two people, each of whom had the advice and assistance of many others. Charles H. Lesser had largely completed the painstaking bibliographical research prior to his appointment as assistant director of archives and publications at the South Carolina Department of Archives and History. The organization of the volume, the addition of the section on personal narratives, and the expansion of the treatment of primary sources, however, as well as all the textual material, are mine alone. Dr. Lesser shares a great deal of the credit for the publication of this Guide, but none of the responsibility for any errors which it may contain. Howard H. Peckham, director of the William L. Clements Library, provided guidance and assistance throughout my tenure with the library's bicentennial project. John Dann offered valuable suggestions, and John Shy was generous with his advice. I would like to thank George Chalou, Kenneth Harris, and Howard Wehmann of the National Archives and Ruth Klein of the National Society of the Daughters of the American Revolution Library. Deborah Lincoln Lockwood, John Irwin, and Tessa White checked bibliographic information, organized files, typed portions of the draft, and performed a variety of tasks in connection with the project.

Christine Vroom typed most of the final copy. Finally, a great deal of appreciation is due Barbara Mitchell, whose editorial skills and devotion to hard work played an essential part in bringing this Guide to completion.

J. Todd White

Library of Congress
National Union Catalog Symbols

BM   British Museum Library, London, England

CaOOHa   Haldimand Collection, Canadian Archives, Ottawa, Ontario, Canada

CSmH   Henry E. Huntington Library, San Marino, Calif.

Ct   Connecticut State Library, Hartford, Conn.

CtCLA   Cornwall Library Association, Cornwall, Conn.

CtHi   Connecticut Historical Society, Hartford, Conn.

CtNhHi   New Haven Colony Historical Society, New Haven, Conn.

CtY   Yale University, New Haven, Conn.

DLC   U.S. Library of Congress, Washington, D.C.

DNA   U.S. National Archives, Washington, D.C.

DNDAR   National Society of the Daughters of the American Revolution Library, Washington, D.C.

GHi   Georgia Historical Society, Savannah, Ga.

ICN   Newberry Library, Chicago, Ill.

KyLoF   Filson Club, Louisville, Ky.

MB   Boston Public Library, Boston, Mass.

MBAt   Boston Athenaeum, Boston, Mass.

MBC   American Congregational Association, Boston, Mass.

MBNEH   New England Historic Genealogical Society, Boston, Mass.

MdHi   Maryland Historical Society, Baltimore, Md.

MeBaHi   Bangor Historical Society, Bangor, Me.

MeHi   Maine Historical Society, Portland, Me.

MH   Harvard University, Cambridge, Mass.

MHi   Massachusetts Historical Society, Boston, Mass.

MiU-C   University of Michigan, William L. Clements Library, Ann Arbor, Mich.

MnHi   Minnesota Historical Society, Saint Paul, Minn.

MoU   University of Missouri, Columbia, Mo.

MSaE   Essex Institute, Salem, Mass.

MTaHi   Old Colony Historical Society, Taunton, Mass.

MWA   American Antiquarian Society, Worcester, Mass.

MWeAt	Westfield Athenaeum, Westfield, Mass.
N	New York State Library, Albany, N.Y.
NBuHi	Buffalo Historical Society, Buffalo, N.Y.
NCanHi	Ontario County Historical Society, Canandaigua, N.Y.
Nc-Ar	North Carolina State Department of Archives and History, Raleigh, N.C.
NCooHi	New York State Historical Association, Cooperstown, N.Y.
NElmHi	Chemung County Historical Society, Elmira, N.Y.
NhHi	New Hampshire Historical Society, Concord, N.H.
NHi	New York Historical Society, New York, N.Y.
NIC	Cornell University, Ithaca, N.Y.
NjHi	New Jersey Historical Society, Newark, N.J.
NjR	Rutgers–The State University, New Brunswick, N.J.
NN	New York Public Library, New York, N.Y.
NNPM	Pierpont Morgan Library, New York, N.Y.
NRHi	Rochester Historical Society, Rochester, N.Y.
NSchHi	Schenectady County Historical Society, Schenectady, N.Y.
NWM	U.S. Military Academy, West Point, N.Y.
OClWHi	Western Reserve Historical Society, Cleveland, Ohio
PHi	Historical Society of Pennsylvania, Philadelphia, Pa.
PPL	Library Company of Philadelphia, Philadelphia, Pa.
RHi	Rhode Island Historical Society, Providence, R.I.
RNHi	Newport Historical Society, Newport, R.I.
SCAr	South Carolina Department of Archives and History, Columbia, S.C.
Vi	Virginia State Library, Richmond, Va.
VtMiS	Sheldon Art Museum, Middlebury, Vt.
WHi	State Historical Society of Wisconsin, Madison, Wis.

1

MILITARY AND
RELATED RECORDS

☆

Historians have long been aware that the American Revolution witnessed a proliferation of legislative documents, personal letters, and political pamphlets. For the most part, however, there has been less awareness of a similar proliferation of records in the military sphere. The creation of national and state military forces and the coordination of a national military effort generated a vast body of administrative documents which contain biographical information on the men who bore arms during the war. Following the disbanding of the revolutionary military forces, the settlement of claims for back pay and the passage of pension legislation extended the creation of military-related documents well into the nineteenth century. The importance of these records, long recognized by the genealogical community, is that they document the lives of ordinary men — and through them their families — for whom there are no collected letters, no pamphlet literature, nor any recognition in the journals of the various revolutionary legislatures or committees.

In many ways military records are similar to tax records, a more traditional source of information on those who made no personal impact on the decisions of government and the movements of armies. Like tax records, military records provide names of individuals and some estimation of their rank in society, military rank being as important an indicator of social standing as the assessed value of an estate. Military records have the added advantage of providing names of men who do not appear in tax records, nor in other early American records which depended largely on possession of property. Many soldiers owned no property or owned too little of it to be taxed. Many others were too young to have established a separate household from their parents. For a large number of men of the revolutionary period, unless their births were recorded, their appearance in the administrative documents of the military conflict is the first record of their existence. For some this is the only record, and for others it is the beginning of a documentation that lasted until the end of their lives.

1

WAR RECORDS

Revolutionary War Rolls

The two most common military documents that contain names are the muster and pay rolls. Muster rolls are essentially an attendance record compiled at the lowest level of military command. They give name, rank, military service organization, and, occasionally, other bits of information. Pay rolls record the fact that a man has been paid for performing military service and include the period of time for which he was paid. The soldier's rank and military service organization can also be determined from the pay roll. Militia pay rolls are particularly interesting. They give the same information that a pay roll for a Continental or state unit includes, but they also tell for what purpose the militia was called out and how long each militiaman was under arms. Very little is known about the service of the local militias, and pay rolls may provide an excellent basis for determining which members of a community served in the militia and how much service was performed in these units. Potentially, much can be learned about grass-roots support of the Revolution through the study of militia participation.

The most valuable document to be found in collections of revolutionary war rolls is the descriptive or size roll. This document, which may appear under various titles, was prepared to prevent multiple enlistment and to aid in the apprehension of deserters by providing a complete description of the soldier. The information on these descriptive rolls varied according to the type of information the compiler thought to be important. There is always some information on the soldier's military service: rank, date and place of enlistment, and the term of service are frequently recorded. There may also be a record of promotions and brief statements explaining the soldier's departure from the regiment or company, such as "never joined," "deserted," "killed," or "discharged," often with the date the event took place.

The descriptive roll also provides information on the soldier's civilian life, which may include his place of birth, place of residence, and civilian occupation. These documents always contain a physical description. The usual entries are for height and for color of hair, eyes, and complexion. Sometimes there is a column for distinguishing physical marks. The soldier's age is frequently given, and on some of these documents a signature or mark was required.

Descriptive rolls do not exist for every unit in the army, nor are they separated from muster or pay rolls in general collections of revolutionary war rolls. Because of their value, however, they are worth searching for. The location of one may be sufficient justification for selecting a particular military unit for study.

Collections of revolutionary war rolls contain several other types of documents as well. There are large numbers of "returns," which are statistical summaries of personnel in military units. In addition, there is a wide variety of miscellaneous lists. Lists of officers are frequent, and lists of prisoners, lists of soldiers whose enlistments were due to expire, and lists of killed and wounded may also be found.

Other Wartime Administrative Documents

The quantity of documentation required for the day-to-day operation of eighteenth-century military forces was extensive. For example, records were kept for practically every type of financial transaction. Many of these record dealings between the army and civilian suppliers and are chiefly valuable for studying the economic impact of the revolutionary war on American society. There is also a large body of documents, such as oaths of allegiance, enlistment papers, court-martial proceedings, and discharges, which record the military service of revolutionary soldiers and sailors.

Account books often contain significant data on individual soldiers and sailors. Among the numbered record books in Record Group 93 at the National Archives can be found such items as "Clothing Accounts of Lt. Charles Russell, Paymaster, 1st Virginia State Regiment, 1779–1780." This account book records the issuance of clothing to enlisted men and the amounts debited from their pay. It is arranged by the names of persons having accounts and contains an index to those names. Although account books tend to duplicate the type of information found in muster and pay rolls, they can provide some record of service where rolls are missing.

A similar type of record, also located in Record Group 93 but not limited to a single regiment, is the "Paymaster General's Record of Money Due to Officers and Men of Connecticut, Massachusetts and New Hampshire Regiments, and to Capt. Robert Walker's Company of Col. John Lamb's Artillery Regiment, 1779–1780." These accounts record amounts of pay due to men missing from their units for reasons ranging from desertion to killed in action. Each entry gives the man's rank and the reason for his absence.

Orderly books, another type of revolutionary war administrative record, were kept at all levels of command through the regiment to record the orders and instructions pertinent to the military unit. As a result, they differ widely in content. Some orderly books contain little more than the general orders issued at headquarters. Others contain general orders, brigade orders, regimental orders, and a log of activities for the unit. These records of daily events, especially the proceedings of courts-martial, often give information on individuals and the units in which they served.

In general, orderly books are best utilized when a military unit has been singled out for study or when an individual or group of individuals under investigation is known to have served in a particular unit. Random searching of orderly books for biographical information on men not known, or at least not strongly suspected, to have served in the units for which the orderly books were kept is seldom worth the effort. Searching for particular orderly books, however, may be worthwhile since large numbers of them have been preserved. The Library of Congress holds approximately ninety of these and the National Archives another seventy. Their presence in state archives and historical societies is widespread.

Petitions

Many civilians began their military careers by petitioning their legislatures or the Continental Congress for officer's commissions. Once appointed, they petitioned for promotions, especially when they felt that someone less deserving or someone who had less seniority had been promoted over them. Finally, officers wishing to leave the army had to request permission to resign their commissions. These various letters and petitions contain a great deal of information for studying the officer corps as a group or for obtaining information on individuals.

There is a large collection of these documents in the *Papers of the Continental Congress* at the National Archives, and resignations in particular may also be found in the *George Washington Papers* at the Library of Congress. Similar documents exist in state legislative records and in the collected papers of other high-ranking officers.

Using the Document Collections

For many years documents like those discussed above have been heavily exploited by the genealogical researcher. In response to this demand, repositories holding such collections have made every effort to make this material available and to facilitate research, particularly the retrieval of information on individuals. This has been accomplished by publishing the documents with indexes and providing the collections with a variety of finding aids or shortcuts to research. Custodians of such documents should always be consulted on the availability of finding aids.

Three separate series in the War Department Collection of Revolutionary War Records (Record Group 93 in the National Archives) may be used to illustrate the availability of finding aids. The three series, *Numbered Record Books*, *Miscellaneous Numbered Records*, and *Revolutionary War Rolls* occupy 106 linear feet and are now published on 304 rolls of microfilm.[1] Despite the fact that these documents have, to some extent, been organized by state and military unit, research in such a large collection would be extremely difficult. Fortunately, there are several finding aids and indexes. First, *Preliminary Inventory No. 144*, revised, covers all of Record Group 93 and includes a description of various finding aids. It notes one highly valuable shortcut to research and two equally useful indexes applicable to the three series under discussion.

Beginning in the 1890s, clerks working in the Record and Pension Office examined all of the documents in the *Revolutionary War Rolls* and parts of the *Numbered Record Books*. A card was prepared which contained all the information about an individual soldier for each document on which his name was found. All cards for an individual soldier were then combined in a "jacket" constituting his "compiled service record." As a result, the necessity of searching the *Revolutionary War Rolls* or parts of the *Numbered Record Books* for the military service record of an individual soldier has been eliminated.

Once the jackets were compiled, they were placed within major divisions, such as Continental Army, state troops, or Navy. Thereunder, arrangement is by military unit and then alphabetical by surname. Thus, research on military units is possible using the *Compiled Service Records*. The search for individual soldiers within the *Compiled Service Records* is facilitated by the *General Index to Compiled Military Service Records* arranged alphabetically. This gives the rank and military organization of the soldier and thereby provides access to the *Compiled Service Records*.

In addition, there is an index to those parts of the *Numbered Record Books* which were not used to create the *Compiled Service Records* and to the large collection of documents in the *Miscellaneous Numbered Records*. In short, research in a very large collection of documents in three separate series has been made practical by the existence of aids

1. Items discussed in the text appear in the alphabetical listings below.

and indexes. Microfilming of the *Compiled Service Records* and the indexes, as well as the three document collections, has increased the availability of the resources. Most of these microfilm publications are accompanied by explanatory pamphlets, which serve as general finding aids, discuss available indexes, and direct scholars to related records. As these three series illustrate, the War Department Collection of Revolutionary War Records in the National Archives is an extensive and sometimes confusing body of documents. But largely in response to the needs of the genealogical researcher, several different and overlapping finding aids have been created.

Although the National Archives possesses what is perhaps the largest collection of revolutionary war documents and the most detailed finding aids, the state archives have experienced a similar demand for their resources from the genealogist. As a result, many have either published their materials or provided similar aids to research. The Pennsylvania Historical and Museum Commission has Military Abstract Cards of service records for all Pennsylvania soldiers in the manuscripts held by the Commission and in the published *Pennsylvania Archives*. The New Jersey State Archives at Trenton and the North Carolina Department of Archives and History have similar card files indexing their collections of revolutionary war records.

POSTWAR RECORDS

Records relating to the men who bore arms during the American Revolution continued to be created after the war was over. The need to remunerate soldiers for back pay, officers' claims for half pay or commutation, the distribution of bounty lands, and the passage of pension legislation combined to document the lives of many soldiers and sailors well into the nineteenth century.

Revolutionary Claims

At the end of the war, both the central government and the individual states owed large debts to soldiers and civilians alike. Behind most of these debts was the breakdown of revolutionary finance, with the result that many servicemen had not been paid. Furthermore, debts were owed to military personnel for depreciation of pay, rations undelivered, invalid and widow's pensions, and half pay for officers or the commutation of half pay into a lump sum. These debts resulted in another large body of documents which can be broken down into three main categories: the claims themselves, official action on those claims, and receipts for money or certificates issued on those claims.

The claims were submitted to the Continental Congress, the Federal Congress, and the state legislatures. In letter or petition form, claimants stated the reasons they believed they were due compensation from the government. For soldiers claiming back pay, half pay, commutation, or any other debt owed for military service, the claims frequently give detailed information on the claimants' service records. Persons filing for invalid pensions stated the nature of their disability and when and where it occurred. Claims for widow's and orphan's benefits provide information on the husband's or father's military service as well as genealogical information. Occasionally, these survivors' claims can provide keys to complex problems created by successive marriages and children by more than one marriage.

Locating specific claims is often difficult. Claims submitted to the Continental Congress may be found through manuscript indexes to the *Papers of the Continental Congress.* A new comprehensive index to these records is nearing completion. It will be an invaluable research aid to those seeking information on specific individuals. Claims presented to the Federal Congresses can be traced through the *Digested Summary and Alphabetical List of Private Claims.*

Official actions on these claims also provide important information. Not only do they show what action the legislature took on the claim, but they often summarize the information in the claim itself. This can be of particular value when the claim itself cannot be located. Examples of this type of material may be found in the *American State Papers.*

Lists of persons acknowledging receipt of money or certificates are, perhaps, more widely known as a genealogical source. "Pierce's Register" has long been a source of the names of men who received certificates from the Continental Congress for sums due as a result of military service. The manuscript of this list, kept by John Pierce, paymaster general of the Continental Army, is in the *Numbered Record Books.* It records the disbursement of approximately 95,000 certificates. This figure does not, however, represent the number of individuals, since soldiers frequently received more than one certificate. A published and alphabetized version of "Pierce's Register" appears in *Seventeenth Report of the National Society of the Daughters of the American Revolution.*

An example of a similar body of records for a single state is the South Carolina *Stub Entries to Indents.* These stub entries resulted from South

Carolina's issuance of vouchers for goods and services during the Revolution, and postwar action by the state to determine its public debt. Each stub entry represents an "indent" given to the holder of a voucher issued during the war. The entry tells to whom the indent was issued, for what reason, and for what amount. Although these records are not limited to payment for military service, many soldiers, including militiamen, are represented. Indeed, considering the near-total dissolution of state government during the British occupation of the South, the stub entry may be the only record of service for a South Carolina soldier.

Bounty Land Records

In return for enlisting in the military service, many soldiers were offered grants of land by both Continental and state authorities. Many claims for bounty land may be found in the type of records discussed immediately above. Others may be found among the federal *Revolutionary War Pension and Bounty-Land-Warrant Application Files* discussed below. There are, however, distinct bodies of records relating to the distribution of bounty lands.

These records are a valuable source of names. They also offer much for a study of social and economic history because it is sometimes possible to ascertain if the soldier deeded his land to another individual. They are not, as might be expected, a particularly good source for studying westward migration. For example, "List of Pennsylvania Officers and Men Entitled to Donation Lands, Feb. 27, 1830," in the *Numbered Record Books*, gives only name, rank, and military organization. Other lists do indicate some disposition of the land grant. "A List of Warrants for Lands Granted, . . ." which is printed in *Roster of Soldiers from North Carolina*, indicates the number of acres in the grant, the number of months the soldier served, and to whom the land was deeded. In many cases, land was deeded to an individual other than the one who performed the service. Colonel Murfree, for example, claimed the land warrants of forty-four different men, a total of approximately 40,000 acres. Many soldiers claimed their own land warrants, but there is no indication that they actually occupied the land granted.

Better methods of tracing westward migration include use of the *Census of Pensioners* and the published pension lists, especially that for 1835. One of the most valuable sources for studying the movement of soldiers after the war, and many other topics as well, is the revolutionary war pension applications.

Revolutionary War Pensions

Revolutionary war pensions are perhaps the most important source of biographical information on soldiers and sailors. For the genealogist, the pension files provide not only vital statistics, but important links between family members and information for tracing the movements of families and individuals. For the historian, there are large quantities of data for studying demographic and family history and for analyzing the composition of the military forces.

The first pension acts were passed during the revolutionary war, but until 1818 they were limited to disabled soldiers or widows and orphans of men killed during the war.[2] By 1818, romanticization of the Revolution and a treasury surplus combined to produce the first of the revolutionary service pension acts not limited to cases involving disability or death. This first act was restricted to men in Continental pay who had served at least nine months or until the end of the war and who were in financial need.

Applications under this act far exceeded the numbers anticipated. Further spurred by the depression of 1819, which wiped out the treasury surplus, Congress sought to exclude those men from the pension rolls who were not truly impoverished. A supplementary act of 1820 required pensioners to submit proof of their financial need. As a result, large numbers of men were removed from the rolls, although many were restored by a subsequent act of 1823.

In 1828 another pension act granted full pay for life to those officers who had been entitled to half pay under the Continental Congress resolution of October 1780. Enlisted personnel who had been granted a bonus of full pay for one year upon discharge by the Continental Congress on 15 May 1778 were also granted full pay for life.

In 1832, the pension rolls were greatly expanded by the passage of an act that extended benefits to all classes of servicemen, militia as well as Continental, who had served for six months. There was no requirement that the applicant demonstrate financial need.

The last important pieces of pension legislation based on revolutionary war service were the several acts respecting widows. The first of these, passed in 1836, granted pensions to the widows of men qualified

2. Additional information on revolutionary war military pensions may be found in William H. Glasson, *Federal Military Pensions in the United States* (New York: Oxford University Press, 1918), pp. 19-97; and in Howard H. Wehmann, Introduction to *National Archives Microfilm Publications, Pamphlet Describing M804, Revolutionary War Pension and Bounty-Land-Warrant Application Files* (Washington, D.C.: National Archives, 1974).

for pensions under the act of 1832 who had been married before the end of the soldier's last period of revolutionary war service. These restrictions were relaxed in stages to the point that a widow was eligible for a pension regardless of the date of her marriage. The last act, passed in 1878, provided a pension for the widow of any soldier who had served as little as two weeks or who had fought in any battle.

The applications for pensions under the various acts discussed above may be found in the *Revolutionary War Pension and Bounty-Land-Warrant Application Files*. These files contain the names of soldiers who applied for bounty lands and invalid pensions, but unless those soldiers also applied under one of the other acts, their files very rarely contain any documents. There are approximately 80,000 pension files, published on 2,670 rolls of microfilm. All applications filed on the basis of a soldier's service are consolidated in a single file. Thus, a file may contain only one application for a soldier or his widow, or it may contain several different applications based on several different acts. The file also contains any supporting data submitted as well as requests for genealogical information and replies to those requests. Each file has been assigned a code — a letter followed by a number. In the current organization of the files the code number has lost meaning and may be safely disregarded except, perhaps, for purposes of citation. The code letter symbols do provide some information. A file containing only a soldier's application is indicated by the letter *S*, which stands for survivor. Widows' applications are noted with the letter *W*, and *R* means rejected. Some caution is necessary in using the letter symbols *W* and *R*. In the early twentieth century, separate files for survivors, widows, and rejected applications were consolidated. As a result, many *W* files also contain the earlier applications of the husbands. Similarly, *R* files may contain one or more accepted applications since *R* usually indicates only that the last application was rejected. In other words, the temptation to use the file designations as the basis for a statistical analysis of the pension files should be avoided.

The application materials in each file are preceded by two additional documents. The first contains the soldier's name and his widow's if she applied for a pension. It also carries the file number discussed above and indicates the state from which the soldier served during the Revolution. The second document — frequently there is more than one of these — represents the official disposition of the application and includes rank, state, military unit, and length of service for the soldier as well as the amount of the pension, and the state in which the pension was collected.

The basic pension application is a narrative deposition given and recorded in a local court. The preamble to the soldier's narrative gives the location of the court, the name of the official receiving the deposition, the date, and the soldier's full name, age, and place of residence. This is followed by the soldier's narrative testimony. Soldiers' applications are concerned with proving military service. Wherever possible, the applicant gave or attempted to give specific details such as the state from which he served, his dates of enlistment and discharge, and the names of the officers under whom he served. This was all that was required, but few applications were confined to such straightforward information. Many contain reasons for enlisting, descriptions of battles and specific events, and any other information that the soldier believed would support his claim that he had served. Often included is an itinerary of the applicant's movements after the war—the places where he lived and for how long. The soldier's narrative is frequently long enough to qualify as a memoir of his military service. Pension files also contain other documents such as testimony from individuals—often other soldiers—which supported the applicant's claim.

The files of all soldiers pensioned under the act of 1818 contain a property schedule unless the pensioner died before the supplementary act of 1820 or failed to meet the requirements for proving financial need. These schedules list everything the soldier owned, from land and buildings to pots and pans, and often contain remarks on the applicant's financial situation with particular emphasis on indebtedness. Names of wives and dependent children also appear frequently.

Widows' applications differ from soldiers' applications in one very important way. Whereas the soldier had to prove that he was in the revolutionary military forces, the widow had to prove that she was married to the man she claimed to be her husband, and when they were married. As a result, widows' applications often contain much of the important genealogical material in the pension application files. The most frequent type of information to be found is proof of marriage. This can be in the form of a sworn statement by a town clerk or local clergyman who extracted the appropriate data from civil or church records; it can be in the form of the deposition of a witness to the marriage ceremony; or, in some cases, it is simply testimony from friends and acquaintances that the man and woman had lived together as husband and wife. Widows' applications also contain names of children with their dates of birth. In general, wives of soldiers were concerned with the civilian aspects of their husbands' lives. The widow's application may tell where she and her husband were born, when and

11

where they met, and when they moved from one place to another. Like the soldiers' applications, those for widows often contain documents supporting the claim for pension. Less often, applications for benefits can be found from survivors other than widows. These too provide genealogical information.

The mere fact that the pension application files allow an important segment of the revolutionary generation to be traced from young adulthood to old age makes them an excellent research source for genealogists and for historians of both the revolutionary period and the early nineteenth century. No caution can diminish their ultimate value, but a few warnings are offered with respect to their use. Very little analysis of these materials has been done. The exact number of files is unknown, and there are no reliable estimates for the number of applications filed under the different acts. It is also not known how many soldiers are represented only by widows' applications. Until such time as the entire body of documents is statistically analyzed, historians should be careful about extending general conclusions to the army as a whole based solely on these documents. For example, the act of 1818 required that the soldier be in financial need. Thus, conclusions with regard to the socio-economic status of the members of the Continental Army, based on the pension files alone, will be biased against those veterans who did not apply because they felt they did not qualify under the financial restrictions of the act.

Another problem one must be aware of is the possibility of fraud. It is a simple fact that some of our revolutionary forebears were not above taking advantage of pensions that they did not deserve. Those who administered the pension acts believed—whether justifiably or not—that many of the petitions contained false information. One thing that may give away a fraudulent claimant is the lack of detail in his application. Some soldiers speak only of major battles and senior officers but mention nothing about their date of enlistment or the name of their company commander. This is not to say that every man who fails to recollect the specifics of his military service was filing a fraudulent claim. Age took its toll on memory as much then as it does now, and many of these men were in their seventies when they filed. Still, those who speak generally of major campaigns under such leaders as Washington and Sullivan—events that were covered in published histories—and offer little definite information on their own service should be viewed with caution.

A further important consideration is the impact of the depression of

1819. Men who were poor in 1820 may not have been so in 1816. Extension of economic status from 1820 back to the Revolution should therefore be done with a degree of care. Like any documentary source, the pension application files should be analyzed with regard to weaknesses as well as strengths, although the merits of these files far outweigh the problems.

The last caveat on the pension files is a technical one. The National Archives has microfilmed two series of pension applications. One is the full series and the other is selected documents only—about one-third of the records. In the latter, few files are filmed in entirety; supporting documents are almost never filmed. While the select series can produce a good picture of the soldier and his family, the full series should be used, wherever possible, to take advantage of the complete documentation.

The pension files themselves are not the only valuable historical and genealogical resource that resulted from the revolutionary war pension program. During the period when the program was actually being administered, several lists of pensioners were compiled. The most extensive of these lists those soldiers receiving pensions as of 1835. This list contains the names of approximately 63,500 revolutionary war pensioners. It is especially useful to those interested in migration patterns because the men are listed by state and county in which they received their pensions. Errors do appear in these lists so that cross checking against the applications is advised.

Revolutionary soldiers and sailors present excellent opportunities for historical and genealogical research. Records have always been kept on military forces, but several factors have combined to make the men who fought for American independence a special case. The breakdown of revolutionary finance, for example, led to the creation of claims through which the life of the serviceman can be traced. The nineteenth-century desire to provide pensions for these men brought about the creation of a body of records which is essentially an oral history. Finally, the interest in these soldiers, especially from the Daughters of the American Revolution, has caused these records to be collected, preserved, organized, indexed, and published. Immediately following is a list of important source collections, both published and microfilmed, which contain biographical information on revolutionary war soldiers and sailors.

1. *Area File of the Naval Records Collections, 1775-1910.* Naval Records Collection of the Office of Naval Records and Library. Record Group 45. National Archives Microfilm Publication M625. 414 rolls.

    Only seventeen rolls of this microfilm publication are applicable to the period of the revolutionary war. There is a card index to names and ships at the National Archives.

2. Brumbaugh, Gaius Marcus. *Revolutionary War Records: Virginia Army and Navy Forces with Bounty Land Warrants for Virginia Military District of Ohio and Virginia Scrip, from Federal and State Archives.* Washington, D.C., 1936. Reprint ed., Baltimore: Genealogical Publishing Co., 1967.

    Approximately 7,100 names. Records arranged randomly, with thorough index.

3. Cartwright, Betty G. C., and Gardiner, Lillian Johnson, comps. *North Carolina Land Grants in Tennessee, 1778-1791.* Memphis: I. C. Harper Co., 1958.

    Approximately 5,800 names of those granted lands on basis of revolutionary war service. Arranged by grant numbers, with index to soldiers, their widows and heirs.

4. *Compiled Service Records of American Naval Personnel and Members of the Department of the Quarter Master General and the Commissary General of Military Stores Who Served during the American Revolution.* War Department Collection of Revolutionary War Records. Record Group 93. National Archives Microfilm Publication M880. 4 rolls. And, *Index to Compiled Service Records of American Naval Personnel Who Served during the Revolutionary War.* War Department Collection of Revolutionary War Records. Record Group 93. National Archives Microfilm Publication M879. 1 roll.

5. *Compiled Service Records of Soldiers Who Served in the American Army during the Revolutionary War.* War Department Collection of Revolutionary War Records. Record Group 93. National Archives Microfilm Publication M881. 1,096 rolls. And, *General Index to Compiled Service Records of Revolutionary War Soldiers.* War Department Collection of Revolutionary War Records. Record Group 93. National Archives Microfilm Publication M860. 58 rolls.

6. Connecticut Adjutant General's Office. *Record of Service of Connecticut Men in the War of the Revolution, War of 1812, Mexican War.* Edited by Henry Phelps Johnston. Hartford, 1889. *See also* 73.

7. Connecticut Historical Society. *Rolls and Lists of Connecticut Men*

in the Revolution, 1775-1783. Lists and Returns of Connecticut Men in the Revolution, 1775-1783. Collections of the Connecticut Historical Society, vols. 8, 12. Hartford, 1901, 1909.

8. Delaware, Public Archives Commission. *Delaware Archives,* vols. 1-3. Wilmington, 1911-19. Reprint ed., New York: AMS Press, 1974.

    Rolls and lists, with some additional military records.

9. Force, Peter, comp. *American Archives.* 4th ser., 6 vols. 5th ser., 3 vols. Washington, D.C., 1837-53.

    Includes a large number of rolls and lists.

10. Georgia, Department of Archives and History. *Revolutionary Soldiers' Receipts for Georgia Bounty Grants.* Atlanta: Foote & Davies Co., 1928.

    Approximately 1,000 names. Limited military service data and whether receipt carried soldier's signature or mark.

11. Georgia, Secretary of State. *Authentic List of All Land Lottery Grants Made to Veterans of the Revolutionary War by the State of Georgia, Taken from Official State Records in the Surveyor-General Department, Housed in the Georgia Department of Archives and History.* Compiled by Alex M. Hitz. Atlanta, 1955.

12. Hammond, Isaac Weare, ed. *Rolls of the Soldiers in the Revolutionary War. Provincial and State Papers of New Hampshire,* vols. 14-17. Concord and Manchester, 1885-89. Reprint ed., New York: AMS Press, 1973. *See also* 53.

13. Houston, Martha Lou, comp. *Reprint of Official Register of Land Lottery of Georgia, 1827.* Columbus, Ga., 1929. Reprint ed., Baltimore: Genealogical Publishing Co., 1967.

    Contains approximately 15,000 names; 1,500 of these are revolutionary war soldiers and so designated in this list.

14. Maryland Historical Society. *Muster Rolls and Other Records of Service of Maryland Troops in the American Revolution, 1775-1783. Archives of Maryland,* vol. 18. Baltimore, 1900.

15. *Miscellaneous Numbered Records (the Manuscript File) in the War Department Collection of Revolutionary War Records, 1775-1790's.* War Department Collection of Revolutionary War Records. Record Group 93. National Archives Microfilm Publication M859. 125 rolls. For index, *see* 30.

    A wide variety of revolutionary war records, including, but not confined to, pay accounts, certificates of nonindebtedness, official and personal correspondence, muster rolls, pension certificates, and petitions.

16. New-York Historical Society. *Muster and Pay Rolls of the War of the Revolution, 1775-1783. Collections of the New-York Historical Society*, vols., 47, 48. New York, 1914-15.

17. New York (State) Secretary of State. *The Balloting Book, and Other Documents Relating to Military Bounty Lands, in the State of New York.* Albany, 1825.

Includes rolls of the First and Second Regiments of the New York line and partial returns of other units, as well as acts relating to the bounty lands and minutes of the commissioners of the land office.

18. ———. *Calendar of Historical Manuscripts Relating to the War of the Revolution, in the Office of the Secretary of State.* 2 vols. Albany, 1868.

Many rolls and lists printed in full.

19. *Numbered Record Books Concerning Military Operations and Service, Pay and Settlement of Accounts, and Supplies in the War Department Collection of Revolutionary War Records.* War Department Collection of Revolutionary War Records. Record Group 93. National Archives Microfilm Publication M853. 41 rolls. For partial index of this item, *see* 30.

Contains extensive lists of soldiers for nine of the original thirteen states, seventy orderly books, and a variety of other records including the receipt books of John Pierce (*see* 86).

20. Palmer, William P., ed. *Calendar of Virginia State Papers and Other Manuscripts ... Preserved in the Capitol*, vols. 1-3. Richmond, 1875-83.

Many rolls and lists printed in full. For indexes, *see* 173 and 336.

21. *Papers of the Continental Congress, 1774-1789.* Records of the Continental and Confederation Congresses and the Constitutional Convention, Record Group 360. National Archives Microfilm Publication M247. 204 rolls.

22. *Pennsylvania Archives.* 2d ser., vols. 1, 3, 8-11, 13-15. 3d ser., vol. 23. 5th ser., vols. 1-8. 6th ser., vols. 1, 2, 15 (index to 5th ser.). 7th ser., vols. 1-5 (index to 6th ser.). Philadelphia, 1874-1914. Described in Henry H. Eddy, comp., *Guide to the Published Archives of Pennsylvania, Covering the 138 Volumes of "Colonial Records" and "Pennsylvania Archives," Series 1-9; with an Alphabetical Finding List and Two Special Indexes.* Harrisburg: Pennsylvania Historical and Museum Commission, 1949.

23. *Personnel Returns of the 6th Massachusetts Battalion, 1779-1780, and Returns and Accounts of Military Stores for the 8th and 9th*

Massachusetts Regiments, 1779-1782. War Department Collection of Revolutionary War Records. Record Group 93. National Archives Microfilm Publication M913. 1 roll.

24. *Revolutionary War Pension and Bounty-Land-Warrant Application Files.* Records of the Veterans Administration. Record Group 15. National Archives Microfilm Publication M804 (complete files, 2,670 rolls) and M805 (selected records, 898 rolls). Indexed in *Index of Revolutionary War Pension Applications in the National Archives.* Bicentennial edition, revised and enlarged (Washington, D. C.: National Genealogical Society, 1976).

> Approximately 80,000 files. All applications relating to a single soldier are together under the last application (e.g., that of a widow) based on his service. The index, an alphabetical list including state in which soldier served, was originally published in the *National Genealogical Society Quarterly,* 1943-64, and first appeared in book form in 1966.

25. *Revolutionary War Rolls.* War Department Collection of Revolutionary War Records. Record Group 93. National Archives Microfilm Publication M246. 138 rolls.

> A large collection of muster and pay rolls, returns, and a great variety of lists. Organization is primarily by state and thereunder by military unit.

26. Salley, A. S., Jr., ed. *Documents Relating to the History of South Carolina during the Revolutionary War.* Columbia: Historical Commission of South Carolina, 1908.

27. Smith, James F. *The Cherokee Land Lottery, Containing a Numerical List of Names of the Fortunate Drawers in Said Lottery.* New York, 1838. Reprint ed., Baltimore: Genealogical Publishing Co., 1969. For index, *see* 211.

> Approximately 20,000 names. Revolutionary war soldiers are indicated.

28. South Carolina Department of Archives and History. *Accounts Audited of Claims Growing out of the Revolution in South Carolina.* South Carolina Department of Archives and History. Microcopy no. 8. In process and nearing completion. Approximately 170 rolls.

> Original indents issued to civilians as well as soldiers against financial obligations for goods and services. The approximately 9,000 files contain petitions for claims and other documentation, which is sometimes extensive. A small fragment of the series was published in letterpress in A. S. Salley, ed., *Accounts Audited of Revo-*

lutionary Claims against South Carolina, 3 vols. Columbia: Historical Commission of South Carolina, 1935-43. *See also* 29.

29. ———. *Stub Entries to Indents Issued in Payment of Claims against South Carolina Growing out of the Revolution*. Edited by A. S. Salley, Jr. (vols. 1-8) and Wylma Anne Wates (vols. 9-12). 12 vols. Columbia, 1910-57.

Arranged by number of entry in original manuscript volumes, with name index in each volume. Entries give date of issuance, amount of claim, and brief description of service rendered. Not all volumes in the series have been published (*see* 28).

30. *Special Index to Numbered Records in the War Department Collection of Revolutionary War Records, 1775-1783*. War Department Collection of Revolutionary War Records. Record Group 93. National Archives Microfilm Publication M847. 39 rolls.

Alphabetical index to names in the photographic copies of state records, the manuscript file (*see* 15), and parts of the numbered record books (*see* 19) in Record Group 93, with citations. Most entries have limited military service data where applicable.

31. United States Bureau of the Census. *A Census of Pensioners for Revolutionary or Military Service; with Their Names, Ages, and Places of Residence*. Washington, D.C., 1841. Reprint ed., Baltimore: Genealogical Publishing Co., 1974. Also available as National Archives Microfilm Publication T498, roll 3. Indexed in Genealogical Society of Church of Jesus Christ of Latter-day Saints, *A General Index to "A Census of Pensioners for Revolutionary or Military Service, 1840."* Baltimore, 1965. Reprint ed., Baltimore: Genealogical Publishing Co., 1974.

By state, county, and place thereunder. Includes head of family with whom pensioner resided. Does not distinguish revolutionary war from other military service.

32. United States Congress. *American State Papers; Documents, Legislative and Executive, of the Congress of the United States, from the First Session of the First to the Second Session of the Seventeenth Congress, Inclusive: Commencing March 4, 1789, and Ending March 3, 1823; Claims Volume*. Edited by Walter Lowrie and Walter S. Franklin. Washington, D.C., 1834.

Contains full text of a large number of reports dealing with the claims of revolutionary veterans, their widows and heirs. Revolutionary items located through index.

33. ———. *List of the Names of Such Officers and Soldiers of the*

Revolutionary Army as Have Acquired a Right to Lands from the United States and Who Have Not Yet Applied Therefor. 20th Cong., 1st sess., 1828, Sen. Doc. 42.

> Approximately 2,600 names with rank only. Main list is arranged by state. Some separate sections for individual units.

34. United States Department of the Interior. *Report of the Secretary of the Interior, with a Statement of Rejected or Suspended Applications for Revolutionary War Pensions.* 32d Cong., 1st sess., 1852, Sen. Exec. Doc. 37. Reprint with added index to states. Baltimore: Genealogical Publishing Co., 1969.

> Approximately 9,200 names, with place of residence at time of application or receipt of pension, and reason for rejection.

35. United States General Land Office. *Report from the Secretary of the Treasury, in Obedience to a Resolution of the Senate of the 16th of June Last, with Statements Showing the Amount of Land Script Issued (Satisfied and Unsatisfied) to the Officers and Soldiers of the Virginia Line and Navy, and of the Continental Army, during the Revolutionary War.* 23d Cong., 2d sess., 1834, Sen. Doc. 4

> Three separate lists with a total of approximately 900 names; rank and whether service was in army or navy.

36. United States House of Representatives. *Digested Summary and Alphabetical List of Private Claims Which Have Been Presented to the House of Representatives from the First to the Thirty-first Congress.* 3 vols. 32d Cong., 1st sess., 1853, House Misc. Doc. Reprint ed., Baltimore: Genealogical Publishing Co., 1970.

> Alphabetical list of approximately 60,000 claimants. State of residence given for some. Includes date of claim; decision in Congress (favorable or unfavorable); and citation to congressional journals, reports, bills, acts, and laws where full text of claim may be found. Compensation, pay, bounty lands, and pensions for revolutionary war service are noted under nature of claims.

37. United States Naval History Division. *Naval Documents of the American Revolution.* Edited by William Bell Clark (vols. 1-4) and William James Morgan (vol. 5-). Washington, D.C.: Government Printing Office., 1964-.

38. United States War Department. *Letter from the Secretary of War, Communicating a Transcript of the Pension List of the United States ... June 1, 1813.* Washington D.C., 1813. Reprint ed., *Revolutionary Pensioners: A Transcript of the Pension List of the United States for 1813.* Baltimore: Genealogical Publishing Co., 1959.

Arranged by state of residence when application was made. Gives rank only for 1,776 pensioners. Revolutionary war service not indicated.

39. ———. *Letter from the Secretary of War, Transmitting a List of the Names of Pensioners, under the Act of 18th of March, 1818, Whose Names Were Struck Off the List by Act of 1st May, 1820, and Subsequently Restored.* Washington, D.C., 1836. Reprint ed., *Pensioners of Revolutionary War—Struck Off the Roll.* Baltimore: Genealogical Publishing Co., 1969.

Approximately 450 names, arranged by state. Gives date of the act by which pensioner was restored.

40. ———. *Letter from the Secretary of War, Transmitting a Report of the Names, Rank, and Line of Every Person Placed on the Pension List, in Pursuance of the Act of 18th March, 1818.* Washington, D.C., 1820. Reprint ed., Baltimore: Genealogical Publishing Co., 1955.

Gives state only, not unit, in which 16,164 pensioners served. Arranged by these pensioners' states of residence at time of application.

41. ———. *Message from the President of the United States, Transmitting a Report of the Secretary of War in Compliance with a Resolution of the Senate, "to cause to be laid before them, a list of all the pensioners of the United States, the sum annually paid to each, and the state or territories in which the said pensioners reside."* Washington, D.C., 1818. Reprint ed., *Revolutionary Pensioners of 1818*, with added index to states. Baltimore: Genealogical Publishing Co., 1959.

Part A has 3,814 pensioners, alphabetically under state or territory with rank. Part B has 2,086 additional pensioners and a list of widows and orphans. Does not distinguish revolutionary war pensioners from others.

42. ———. *Report from the Secretary of War, in Obedience to Resolutions of the Senate of the 5th and 30th of June, 1834, and the 3d of March, 1834, and the 3d of March, 1835, in Relation to the Pension Establishment of the United States.* 3 vols. 23d Cong., 1st sess., 1834, Sen. Doc. 514. Reprint ed., *The Pension Roll of 1835.* Baltimore: Genealogical Publishing Co., 1968.

Approximately 63,500 names of revolutionary war pensioners. Volumes are by regions, divided thereunder by states. Rank, sums received, date when placed on pension roll, age, and date of death; service data limited to such brief descriptions as "Massachusetts line"; the most extensive published pension roll.

43. Vermont, Legislature. *Rolls of Soldiers in the Revolutionary War, 1775-1783.* Compiled and edited by John E. Goodrich. Rutland: Tuttle Co., 1904.

44. *Virginia Half Pay and Other Related Revolutionary War Pension Application Files.* Records of the Veterans Administration. Record Group 15. National Archives Microfilm Publication M910. 18 rolls. Files for 279 applicants, arranged by soldiers, then sailors and alphabetically thereunder. The main series of pension applications (*see* 24) has files related to most of these men and also includes Virginia half pay claims that are not in these files.

2

COMPILED LISTS OF NAMES
AND BIOGRAPHICAL SKETCHES

☆

The vast quantity of biographical information in primary sources has been used as the basis for a large number and wide variety of works. In size these compilations range from the seventeen-volume *Massachusetts Soldiers and Sailors of the Revolutionary War* to E. B. Hilliard's *Last Men of the Revolution*, which treats only seven men. In scope they range from the very full biographical sketches contained in *Memorials of the Massachusetts Society of the Cincinnati* to the simple list of names in the Society of Old Brooklynites' list of men incarcerated on the British prison ship *Jersey*.

Most of the entries in the bibliography which follows are annotated. Where annotation is lacking, it is either because the title is sufficiently descriptive, or because the work was not examined and the source for the citation did not provide data on which to base an annotation. Wherever possible, annotations indicate the number of names or biographical sketches included and the type of information given in each work. The location of typescripts is indicated by Library of Congress National Union Catalog symbols following the entries. A list of these symbols may be found in the front of this book.

No attempt has been made to judge the quality of the works listed. Although sources can be identified for many of the compilations listed below, and some even include specific source citations for each entry, checking those sources against the compiled data to confirm reliability would have been prohibitively time-consuming. In other compilations, only general statements are given about the sources of information, and in a few, there is no indication at all about the materials used in compiling the work. Furthermore, a good portion of these works are based, wholly or in part, on archaeological research, particularly the investigation of graveyards. In short, though no item has been included which was recognized as totally unreliable, judgment about the quality of these works remains with those who use them.

45. Alabama Department of Archives and History. *Revolutionary Soldiers in Alabama, Being a List of Names Compiled from Authentic Sources, of Soldiers of the American Revolution, Who Resided in the State of Alabama.* Montgomery: Brown Printing Co., 1911. Reprint ed., Baltimore: Genealogical Publishing Co., 1967.

    Approximately 500 biographies with personal and military service data.

46. Allen, Gardner Weld. *Massachusetts Privateers of the Revolution. Collections of the Massachusetts Historical Society,* vol. 77. Boston, 1927.

    Contains lists of privateers with commanders, owners, and bondsmen. No crew lists.

47. ———. *A Naval History of the American Revolution.* Boston and New York: Houghton Mifflin, 1913.

    Appendixes include lists of vessels and names of Continental Navy officers.

48. "American Prisoners in Mill Prison at Plymouth, [England], in 1782; Captain Green's Letter." *South Carolina Historical and Genealogical Magazine* 10 (1909):116-24.

    List of approximately 225 names with rank and state of residence.

49. Armstrong, Zella, comp. *Some Tennessee Heroes of the Revolution Compiled from Pension Statements.* Chattanooga: Lookout Publishing Co., 1933.

    Six pamphlets containing abstracts of vital data from pension applications. Last number has abstracts of applications by widows whose husbands had not been pensioned and an index to all pamphlets.

50. ———. *Twenty-four Hundred Tennessee Pensioners of the Revolution, War of 1812.* Chattanooga: Lookout Publishing Co., 1937.

    A compilation from pension lists. Service organization, residence, and age.

51. Balch, Thomas. *The French in America during the War of Independence, 1777-83.* 2 vols. Philadelphia, 1891-95. Reprint ed., Boston: Gregg Press, 1972.

    Volume 2 contains a list of approximately 1,000 French officers. Content of entries varies widely; many have vital statistics and military service data.

52. Banks, Charles Edward. "Partial List of Men in the Rhode Island Companies of Arnold's Expedition." *Magazine of History,* extra no. 50.

Approximately 155 names with limited military service data.

53. Batchellor, Albert Stillman, ed. *Miscellaneous Revolutionary Documents of New Hampshire. Provincial and State Papers of New Hampshire*, vol. 30. Manchester, 1910.

A variety of lists: Association Test list for New Hampshire, alphabetical list of New Hampshire men located in *Massachusetts Soldiers and Sailors* (*see* 181); pension lists; and miscellaneous war rolls not included in volumes 14–17 of this series (*see* 12).

54. Battey, George Magruder, III. "The Tennessee 'Bee-Hive'; or, Early (1778–1791) N.C. Land Grants in the Volunteer State, Being an Index with Some 3,100 Names of Revolutionary Soldiers and Settlers Who Participated in the Distribution of More Than 5,000,000 Acres of Land." Typescript. Washington, 1949. DLC.

Index to a manuscript volume concerning cession of North Carolina lands to United States. Names and very brief description of land grant site.

55. Beauchamp, William Martin. *Revolutionary Soldiers Resident or Dying in Onondaga County, N.Y., with Supplementary List of Possible Veterans Based on a Pension List of Franklin H. Chase, Syracuse, N.Y. Publications of the Onondaga Historical Association.* Syracuse, 1913. Supplements: 1914, pp. 188–214; 1916, pp. 240–41; 1922, pp. 242–47.

Approximately 1,000 biographical sketches of varying length. Most contain vital statistics.

56. Bellas, Henry Hobart. *A History of the Delaware State Society of the Cincinnati from Its Organization to the Present Time; to Which Is Appended a Brief Account of the Delaware Regiments in the War of the Revolution, also Personal Memoirs of the Officers, Rolls of Same.* Wilmington: Historical Society of Delaware, 1895.

Appendix contains 37 biographical sketches of Delaware members of the Cincinnati with vital statistics and extensive military service data. Also, lists of approximately 160 Delaware officers by military organization with rank and date of commission.

57. Benson, Adolph B. *Sweden and the American Revolution.* New Haven: Tuttle, Morehouse & Taylor Co., 1926.

Includes sixty-four biographies of Swedish officers serving with French or Americans, some of whom did not serve in America. Vital statistics and military service data are occasionally given.

58. Blair, Anna, comp. "A List of Revolutionary Soldiers Buried in

North Carolina." *Historical Collections of the Georgia Chapters, Daughters of the American Revolution* 1 (1926):352-64.

59. Boddie, William Willis. *Marion's Men: A List of Twenty-five Hundred*. Charleston, S.C.: Heisser Printing Co., 1938.

Alphabetical list by rank. Source citations.

60. Bowman, John Elliot, comp. "Some Veterans of the American Revolution in Various Parts of United States; Items from Newspapers, 1816-1850; about 1,500 Items Alphabetically Arranged." Manuscript. New Ipswich, N.H., 1923. DLC.

Extracts from newspaper obituaries. Entries give name, age at death, occasional remarks, and name and date of newspaper from which the item was extracted. A number of similar unpublished items by Bowman may be found in the *National Union Catalog, Pre-1956 Imprints*.

61. Burgess, Louis A., comp. and ed. *Virginia Soldiers of 1776, Compiled from Documents on File in the Virginia Land Office; Together with Material Found in the Archives Department of the Virginia State Library and Other Reliable Sources*. 3 vols. Richmond: Richmond Press, 1927-29. Reprint ed., Spartanburg, S.C.: Reprint Co., 1973.

Abstracts from bounty records in the Virginia Land Office and elsewhere. Some limited service data and names of descendants who claimed bounty lands.

62. Burns, Annie (Walker), comp. "Record of Revolutionary War Pension Papers of Soldiers Who Settled in Kentucky Counties: Adair County, Columbia, Kentucky." Typescript. Wallins Creek, Ky., 1933. DLC.

Burns was a prolific copyist and abstractor of local records. This is 1 of approximately 600 items she compiled, most of which are unpublished. Among these are many abstracts of pension applications and lists of pensioners. Kentucky is emphasized but there are several items for other southeastern states and some for Ohio. A full list of Burns's works may be found in the *National Union Catalog, Pre-1956 Imprints* under the heading Burns, Annie (Walker). Elsewhere Burns may be found listed as Bell, Annie (Walker) Burns.

63. Callahan, Edward W. *List of Officers of the Navy of the United States and of the Marine Corps, from 1775 to 1900, Comprising a Complete Register of All Present and Former Commissioned, Warranted, and Appointed Officers ... Regular and Volunteer; Com-*

piled from the Official Records of the Navy Dept. New York: L. R.
Hamersly & Co., 1901.

64. Campbell, James W. S. *Digest and Revision of Stryker's Officers
and Men of New Jersey in the Revolutionary War for the Use of the
Society of Cincinnati in the State of New Jersey . . . and a List of
Members, with an Exhibit of Delinquent Members of the Society.*
New York: Williams Printing Co., 1911.

Officers only. Information limited to military service data, extensive at time. Promotion records receive special attention. *See* 236.

65. Chamberlain, George Walter. "Revolutionary Soldiers of York
County, Maine." *New England Historical and Genealogical Register*
65 (1911):76-82, 107-15, 254-64, 333-42.

Vital statistics and genealogical data extracted from pension
records.

66. ———. *Soldiers of the American Revolution, of Lebanon, Maine.*
Weymouth, Mass., 1897.

Ninety-five biographical sketches with vital statistics, military
service, and genealogical data.

67. "Chaplains of the French Navy in American Waters." *American
Catholic Researches* 7 (1911):250-57.

One hundred sixty names with limited service data and occasional
date of death.

68. Clark, Alzamore H., ed. *A Complete Roster of Colonel David
Waterbury Jr.'s Regiment of Infantry Responding to a Call for
Volunteers for the Defence of New York City against the British in the
American Revolution; Now for the First Time Printed from Manu-
script Records in the Possession of the Publisher.* New York: A. S.
Clark, 1897.

A list of names by company and thereunder by rank. Extracted
from a manuscript orderly book.

69. Clark, Lewis H. *Military History of Wayne County, [N.Y.]: The
County in the Civil War.* Sodus, N.Y., 1883.

Chapter 5 contains notices of revolutionary war soldiers in Wayne
County, N.Y. Information given varies with the individual soldier
but may include limited military service or genealogical data and
vital statistics. Approximately 300 men included.

70. Clark, Walter, ed. "Roster of the Continental Line from North
Carolina." *State Records of North Carolina* 16:1002-1197.

Alphabetical list of approximately 4,800 soldiers by military unit
with limited military service data.

71. Coburn, Frank Warren. *The Battle of April 19, 1775, in Lexington, Concord, Lincoln, Arlington, Cambridge, Somerville, and Charlestown, Massachusetts.* Special limited edition. Lexington, Mass.: privately printed, 1912. 2d ed. rev. Lexington, Mass.: Lexington Historical Society, 1922.

    Special edition contains a list of 3,600 men who turned out for the Lexington Alarm. Second edition includes a compiled roll of 77 men in Capt. John Parker's company but does not contain the extensive list given in the special edition.

72. Collier, Thomas S. *Revolutionary Privateers of Connecticut, with Accounts of State Cruisers. Records and Papers of the New London County Historical Society*, vol. 1, pt. 4. New London, 1892.

73. Connecticut Adjutant General's Office. *Record of Service of Connecticut Men in the War of the Revolution.* Edited by Henry Phelps Johnston. Hartford, 1889.

    Several different lists in alphabetical order by military unit and rank. Compiled from Connecticut revolutionary war documents. Index has approximately 30,000 name entries.

74. Contenson, Ludovic Guy Marie du Bessey de. *La Société des Cincinnati de France et la guerre d'Amérique, 1778-1783; ouvrage orné de 193 portraits et 17 planches.* Paris: Auguste Picard, 1934.

    Biographical sketches of the original members of the French chapter of the Society of Cincinnati.

75. Cowell, Benjamin. *Spirit of '76 in Rhode Island; or, Sketches of the Efforts of the Government and People in the War of the Revolution together with the Names of Those Who Belonged to Rhode Island Regiments in the Army, with Biographical Notices, Reminiscences, &c., &c.* Boston, 1850. Indexed in James N. Arnold, "Cowell's 'Spirit of '76': An Analytical and Explanatory Index." *Vital Records of Rhode Island* 12 (1901):354-560. Reprint ed., with Arnold's index. Baltimore: Genealogical Publishing Co., 1973.

    Various lists and documents incorporated in a patriotic narrative. Extensive list of officers and men in the Rhode Island regiments. Arnold's index is essential to an easy exploitation of this work.

76. Cox, William E. "Battle of Kings Mountain Participants, October 7, 1780." Reproduced typescript. N.p., n.d. DLC.

    List of 1,166 names with county and state of residence. Compiler states this figure is high. Suspect entries are indicated.

77. Crimmins, John D. "Patriots Bearing Irish Names Who Were

Confined Aboard the *Jersey* Prison Ship." *Journal of the American-Irish Historical Society* 6 (1906):21-30.

A list of men with Irish surnames extracted from a published list of 8,000 men confined on board British prison ships. *See also* 221.

78. Crockett, Walter H. "Soldiers of the Revolutionary War Buried in Vermont, and Anecdotes and Incidents Relating to Some of Them." *Proceedings of the Vermont Historical Society,* 1903-4, pp. 93-106, 114-65; 1905-6, pp. 189-203.

Various lists containing approximately 6,300 names. Two lists of approximately 3,700 soldiers buried in Vermont and lists of pensioners are included. Names are grouped by town or county and thereunder in alphabetical order. Rank is given for commissioned and noncommissioned officers. There are "anecdotes" for only about 85 men. Most of these are short notes on battles in which the individuals participated.

79. Custer, Milo, comp. *Soldiers of the Revolution and the War of 1812 Buried in McLean County, Illinois.* Bloomington, Ind., 1912. Reprint ed., Bloomington, Ind.: Bloomington-Normal Genealogical Society, 1969.

A list of thirteen names with vital statistics and limited military service data for some of them.

80. Dandridge, Mrs. Danske (Bedinger). *American Prisoners of the Revolution.* Charlottesville, Va.: Michie Co., 1911. Reprint ed., Baltimore: Genealogical Publishing Co., 1967.

Appendix A contains a list of 8,000 men incarcerated on the prison ship *Jersey. See also* 221.

81. Daughters of the American Revolution, National Society. *Daughters of the American Revolution Magazine.* July 1892-. Index, vols. 17-71. Genealogical index for vols. 1-84.

Initial publication in 1892 as *The American Monthly Magazine.* Contains many different lists and a variety of information on revolutionary war soldiers. Valuable material may frequently be found in "The Genealogical Department."

82. ———. *DAR Patriot Index.* Washington, D.C.: DAR, 1966. Supplement. Washington, D.C., 1969.

Not an index, but a list of all soldiers and civilian patriots identified by DAR from 1890 to 1966. Over 105,000 names, frequently with vital statistics and brief military service data. Supplement gives similar data for an additional 1,200 names and additions and corrections to the main index.

83. ——. *Index to the Rolls of Honor (Ancestor's Index) in the Lineage Books.* 4 vols. Pittsburgh and Washington, D.C., 1916-40. Reprint ed., Baltimore: Genealogical Publishing Co., 1972.

Four separate indexes to the names of revolutionary ancestors in the DAR *Lineage Books.* Each volume covers a forty-volume segment of the *Lineage Books.* Each volume contains approximately 25,000 index entries, but there is considerable duplication. Rank and state of service is sometimes given with the index entry. *See also* 84.

84. ——. *Lineage Book.* 166 vols. Washington, D.C., 1890-1939.

A list of DAR members in order of National Society membership number. Each entry contains a genealogy back to the revolutionary soldier or civilian patriot. Limited military service data and vital statistics given for each soldier. Each volume contains an index to ancestors. These volumes cover DAR membership only to 1921. *See also* 83.

85. ——. *Report.* Washington, D.C.: Government Printing Office, 1899-.

Beginning with *The Sixteenth Report* (1912-13) this publication contains grave lists of revolutionary military personnel. Over 54,000 grave sites have been located. Soldiers are listed in alphabetical order within each volume. Where known, vital statistics and limited service data are given.

86. ——. *The Seventeenth Report* (1913-14). Washington, D.C.: Government Printing Office, 1915.

Contains an alphabetized version of Pierce's register of certificates disbursed to men who had been in Continental pay and were owed money at the end of the war. Name and certificate number only. Register lists over 93,000 certificates, but this figure exceeds the number of names because one person often received several certificates. *See also* 19.

87. ——. *The Twenty-first Report* (1917-18). Washington, D.C.: Government Printing Office, 1919.

Contains a list of approximately 11,000 pension applicants from Connecticut. Name and pension file number only.

88. Daughters of the American Revolution, Connecticut; Mary Floyd Talmadge Chapter, Litchfield. *Honor Roll of Litchfield County Revolutionary Soldiers.* Edited by Josephine Ellis Richards. Litchfield: DAR, 1912.

Alphabetical list of approximately 4,500 names by town. Source citations.

89. Daughters of the American Revolution. Georgia. "Histories of Revolutionary Soldiers Contributed by Georgia Chapters." 2 vols. Typescript. 1970. DNDAR.

Contains 505 individual biographies with vital statistics, extensive genealogical data, and limited military service data.

90. Daughters of the American Revolution, Indiana. *Roster of Soldiers and Patriots of the American Revolution Buried in Indiana.* Compiled by Mrs. Roscoe C. O'Byrne. Brookville, Ind.: DAR, 1938. Reprint ed., Baltimore: Genealogical Publishing Co., 1968.

Alphabetical list of approximately 1,400 names with vital statistics, genealogical information, and limited military service data. Source citations. *See also* 243.

91. Daughters of the American Revolution, Maine. *Maine Revolutionary Soldiers' Graves.* Augusta: DAR, 1940.

92. ———. *Roster and Ancestral Roll, Maine Daughters of the American Revolution, and the List of Maine Soldiers at Valley Forge, 1777–1778.* Compiled by Mrs. Percy L. Tate. Farmington, 1948.

93. Daughters of the American Revolution, Massachusetts; Col. Timothy Bigelow Chapter, Worcester. *A List of the Soldiers in the War of the Revolution, from Worcester, Mass., with a Record of Their Death and Place of Burial.* Compiled by Mary Cochran Dodge. Worcester: DAR, 1902.

Two separate lists. Name, with date and place of death.

94. Daughters of the American Revolution, Mississippi. *Family Records: Mississippi Revolutionary Soldiers.* Compiled by Alice Tracy Welch. Baltimore: Genealogical Publishing Co., 1956.

Extensive biographical information, including vital statistics, genealogical data, and limited military service data, for approximately 420 soldiers.

95. Daughters of the American Revolution, New Hampshire; Ashuelot Chapter, Keene. *Keene's Revolutionary Soldiers and the House Whence They Started for Lexington.* Keene, 1897.

96. Daughters of the American Revolution, New York; Chautauqua County Chapters. *Soldiers of the American Revolution Who at One Time Were Residents of, or Whose Graves Are Located in Chautauqua County, New York.* Westfield, 1925.

Vital statistics and military service data for approximately 225 soldiers. Listed by contributing DAR chapter and thereunder in alphabetical order.

97. Daughters of the American Revolution, New York; Hendrick Hudson Chapter, Hudson. *Revolutionary War Veterans Buried in Columbia County, New York*. Compiled by Esther Griswold French. Hudson: DAR, 1973.

Vital statistics, military service, and genealogical data for 309 soldiers and civilian patriots. Source citations.

98. Daughters of the American Revolution, New York; Olean Chapter. "Revolutionary Soldiers Buried in Cattaraugus County, New York." Compiled by Julia G. Pierce and Maud D. Brooks. Reproduced typescript. Olean, 1947. DLC.

Vital statistics, military service, and pension data for approximately 120 men. Alphabetical list with source citations.

99. Daughters of the American Revolution, New York; Oneida Chapter, Utica. *Memorial to Revolutionary Soldiers, Clinton, New York*. Utica: Dodge Print, 1938.

Vital statistics and military service data for forty-nine men. Supplemental lists have an additional forty-four names of men not included in the main list. Information in supplemental lists less complete. Source citations.

100. Daughters of the American Revolution, New York; Tawasentha Chapter, Slingerlands. *Pilgrimages to the Graves of 126 Revolutionary Soldiers in the Towns of Guilderland, New Scotland, and Bethleham, Albany County, New York*. Albany: Evory Press, 1940.

Four "pilgrimages," or guided tours, to the grave sites of 126 soldiers. Vital statistics, limited genealogical and military service data.

101. Daughters of the American Revolution, North Carolina. *Roster of Soldiers from North Carolina in the American Revolution: With an Appendix Containing a Collection of Miscellaneous Papers*. Durham: DAR, 1932. Reprint ed., Baltimore: Genealogical Publishing Co., 1972.

A large number of compilations from previously published lists, for example, Heitman's *Register* (*see* 149); from manuscript sources, for example, North Carolina army accounts; and from pension rolls. Index contains approximately 18,000 names.

102. Daughters of the American Revolution, Ohio; Cuyahoga Portage Chapter, Akron. *Revolutionary Soldiers of Summit County and Membership Roll*. Compiled by Mrs. Minnie Weston Franz. Akron: Commercial Printing Co., 1911.

Vital statistics and limited military service data for approximately fifty men. Many entries contain information on migration to Ohio.

103. Daughters of the American Revolution, Ohio; Marietta Chapter. *Revolutionary Soldiers Buried in Washington County, Ohio, Containing Military Record and Short History of Lives.* N.p., 1923.

104. Daughters of the American Revolution, Ohio; New Connecticut Chapter, Painesville. *A Record of the Revolutionary Soldiers Buried in Lake County, Ohio, with a Partial List of Those in Geauga County, and a Membership Roll.* Columbus: Champlin Press, 1902.

105. Daughters of the American Revolution, Pennsylvania; Erie County Chapters. *Soldiers of the American Revolution Who at Some Time Were Residents of, or Whose Graves Are Located in, Erie County, Pennsylvania.* Erie, 1929.

106. Daughters of the American Revolution, Pennsylvania; Franklin County Chapter, Chambersburg. *American Revolutionary Soldiers of Franklin County.* Compiled by Virginia Shannon Fendrick. Chambersburg: DAR, 1944.

107. Daughters of the American Revolution, Pennsylvania; Merion Chapter, Bala. *Revolutionary Soldiers' Graves in Lower Merion Township, Montgomery County, Pennsylvania, and the Surrounding Townships of Roxborough and Blockley, in Philadelphia County; Haverford and Radnor, in Delaware County; and Upper Merion and White Marsh, in Montgomery County.* Bala, 1906.

108. Daughters of the American Revolution, Pennsylvania; Shikelimo Chapter, Lewisburg. *Revolutionary Soldiers' List.* Compiled by Mrs. W. C. Bartol. Lewisburg: Saturday News Print, 1926.

109. Daughters of the American Revolution, South Carolina. *Records of Revolutionary War Soldiers Buried in South Carolina.* Compiled by Mrs. Fred. C. Hensley. 1967–70. Microfilmed cards in the South Caroliniana Library, University of South Carolina, Columbia.

Vital statistics and military service data for approximately 275 men.

110. Daughters of the American Revolution, Tennessee. *Tennessee Soldiers in the Revolution: A Roster of Soldiers Living during the Revolutionary War in the Counties of Washington and Sullivan; Taken from the Revolutionary Army Accounts of North Carolina.* Bristol, Tenn.: DAR, 1935.

Index to North Carolina army accounts in State Archives, Raleigh. Approximately 1,500 names. Separate list of approximately 25 pensioners residing in Tennessee.

111. Davis, Charles Luken. *A Brief History of the North Carolina Troops on the Continental Establishment in the War of the Revolu-*

tion, with a Register of Officers of the Same; also a Sketch of the North Carolina Society of the Cincinnati. Philadelphia, 1896.

Approximately 500 officers by rank and thereunder in alphabetical order. Limited military service data and occasional date of death. The essay on the North Carolina Cincinnati contains one short list of approximately 65 names with rank only.

112. Dawson, Francis Warrington. *Les Français Morts pour l'indépendence américaine de Septembre 1781 à Août 1782 et la reconstruction historique de Williamsburg, base des armées de Rochambeau en Virginie.* Paris: Editions de l'Œuvre latine, 1931.

Contains "La Liste des Français Morts en Virginie de Septembre 1781 à Août 1782." By regiment in alphabetical order with vital statistics and occasional notation that a soldier was conscripted.

113. Dedham Historical Society. *A List of Revolutionary Soldiers Who Served Dedham in the Revolution, 1775-1783.* Dedham, Mass.: Dedham Historical Society, 1917.

Name-only list of 678 soldiers. Most extracted from *Massachusetts Soldiers and Sailors* (*see* 181).

114. Derby, Samuel Carroll. *Early Dublin: A List of the Revolutionary Soldiers of Dublin, N.H.* Columbus, Ohio, 1901.

Approximately 100 entries in 3 separate lists. Content varies, with military service data emphasized; most entries contain vital statistics.

115. DeSaussure, Wilmot G. "The Names ... of the Officers Who Served in the South Carolina Regiments, on the Continental Establishment; of the Officers Who Served in the Militia, of What Troops Were upon the Continental Establishment and of What Militia Organizations Served, Together with Some Miscellaneous Information." Charleston, S.C., *Yearbook*, 1893, pp. 205-37.

116. Dorman, John Frederick, comp. *Virginia's Revolutionary Pension Applications, Abstracted.* Washington, D.C., 1958-.

Detailed abstracts of genealogical data. Well indexed.

117. Draper, Mrs. Amos G. "South Carolina's Revolutionary Soldiers." *Daughters of the American Revolution Magazine*, vols. 42, 43 (1913).

Alphabetical list with very brief phrase relating to military service. List ran serially for ten months only; discontinued at Cuthbert, John.

118. Duncan, Louis C. *Medical Men in the American Revolution, 1775-1783.* Army Medical Bulletin, no. 25. Carlisle Barracks, Pa.: Medical Field Service School, 1931.

Appendix contains a list of approximately 1,400 names. Limited military service data.

119. Egle, William Henry. *Some Pennsylvania Women during the War of the Revolution.* Harrisburg, 1898. Reprint ed., *Pennsylvania Women during the War of the Revolution.* Cottonport, La.: Polyanthos, 1972.

Biographical sketches of sixty-nine women. Some vital statistics. Information on husband's military service. Mostly patriotic narrative.

120. Elliott, Katherine B., comp. "Revolutionary War Records, Mecklenburg County, Virginia." Reproduced typescript. South Hill, Va., 1964. DLC.

Approximately 1,000 names of revolutionary soldiers and civilian patriots. At least one-half are civilians. Vital statistics and military service data. Some entries contain information on soldier's migration following the war. Extensive use of manuscript sources with citations.

121. Ely, Selden Marvin. "The District of Columbia in the American Revolution and Patriots of the Revolutionary Period Who Are Interred in the District or in Arlington." *Records of the Columbia Historical Society* 21 (1918):129–54.

Approximately 250 entries. Grave sites for forty-one soldiers. Limited military service data and occasional birth or death dates.

122. English, William Hayden. *Conquest of the Country Northwest of the River Ohio, 1778–1783, and Life of Gen. George Rogers Clark.* Indianapolis and Kansas City, 1896.

Includes list of Clark's soldiers who were granted land in Indiana.

123. Eno, Joel N. "Irish Revolutionary Soldiers in New York State and Elsewhere." *Americana* 21 (1927):631–38.

Contains a list of approximately 660 soldiers with Irish surnames extracted from *New York in the Revolution* (see 195; see also 125).

124. Ervin, Sara Sullivan, ed. *South Carolinians in the Revolution, with Service Records and Miscellaneous Data, Also Abstracts of Wills, Laurens Co. (Ninety-Six District), 1775–1855.* Ypsilanti [?], Mich., 1949. Reprint ed., Baltimore: Genealogical Publishing Co., 1971.

A compendium of previously published lists. An attempt to include all published material on South Carolina soldiers in one volume. Index contains approximately 2,500 names.

125. Fernow, Berthold, ed. *New York State Archives; New York in the Revolution. Documents Relating to the Colonial History of the State*

of New York, vol. 15. Albany, 1887. Reprint ed., Cottonport, La.: Polyanthos, 1972.

> Contains "Roster of the State Troops." Approximately 34,000 names in alphabetical order with rank and military organization. Another lengthy list of men by military unit and thereunder in alphabetical order with limited military service data, frequently including date and duration of enlistment.

126. Flagg, Charles Alcott. *An Alphabetical Index of Revolutionary Pensioners Living in Maine*. Dover, Me., 1920. Reprint ed., Baltimore: Genealogical Publishing Co., 1967.

> Approximately 3,500 Maine pensioners from published pension lists in alphabetical order with date of pension list; age at time pension list compiled; very general statement of military organization, e.g., Massachusetts line; rank; and residence at time pension list compiled.

127. Flower, Dennis. *Hartland in the Revolutionary War; Her Soldiers; Their Homes, Lives, and Burial Places; the Muster Rolls of Captain Elias Weld's and Lieutenant Daniel Spooner's Hartland Companies; also Hartland in the War of 1812 and in the Mexican War*. Hartland, Vt.: Solitarian Press, 1914.

> List of approximately 150 names with date of death, age at death, and place of interment. Additional information on some of these men is in a separate section.

128. France, Ministère des affaires étrangères. *Les Combattants français de la guerre américaine 1778–1783*. Paris: Ancienne Maison Quantin, 1903. Also, Washington, D.C.: Imprimerie Nationale, 1905. Reprint ed., Baltimore: Genealogical Publishing Co., 1969.

> Approximately 45,000 names of French participants in the revolutionary war. Approximately 80 percent classified as naval personnel. Limited service data. The 1905 edition and the 1969 reprint contain English translations of introductory material and regimental histories as well as a name index.

129. Gardiner, Asa B. *The Order of the Cincinnati in France ("L'Ordre de Cincinnatus"); Its Origin and History: With the Military or Naval Records of the French Members Who Became Such by Reason of Qualifying Service in the Army or Navy of France or of the United States in the War of the Revolution for American Independence*. Providence: Rhode Island Society of the Cincinnati, 1905.

> Approximately 250 biographical sketches of varying length. High-ranking officers only. Extensive military service and biographical data.

130. Gardner, Frank A. [Massachusetts Regiments in the War of the Revolution.] *The Massachusetts Magazine.* Salem, 1908-17.

A series, scattered through this magazine, of short histories of Massachusetts regiments, with some lists and biographical sketches of officers.

131. Gilmore, George C. *The Last Fourteen Survivors of the Revolutionary Army.* Concord, N.H., 1898.

Vital statistics.

132. ———. "New Hampshire Men at Bunker Hill." In New Hampshire, Secretary of State, *Manual for the General Court*, no. 6, pp. 29-86. Manchester, 1899.

Approximately 1,750 names in four separate lists. Limited military service data.

133. ———. *Roll of New Hampshire Soldiers at the Battle of Bennington, August 16, 1777.* Manchester, 1891.

List of approximately 1,500 names with place of residence and limited military service data.

134. Godfrey, Carlos E. *The Commander-in-Chief's Guard; Revolutionary War.* Washington, D.C.: Stevenson-Smith Co., 1904. Reprint ed., Baltimore: Genealogical Publishing Co., 1972.

Extensive military service data for over 300 men. Some entries contain vital statistics and genealogical information.

135. Goold, Nathan. "Col. Edmund Phinney's 18th Continental Regt.; One Year's Service, Commencing January 1, 1776." *Collections and Proceedings of the Maine Historical Society*, 2d ser. 9:45-106.

This item and the three immediately following are among the few genuine regimental histories of the revolutionary war. Biographical sketches of officers and rolls of enlisted men.

136. ———. "Col. James Scammon's 30th Regt. of Foot, 1775." *Collections and Proceedings of the Maine Historical Society*, 2d ser. 10:337-402.

137. ———. "Colonel Jonathan Mitchell's Cumberland County Regt.; Bagaduce Expedition, 1779." *Collections and Proceedings of the Maine Historical Society*, 2d ser. 10:52-80, 143-74.

138. ———. "History of Col. Edmund Phinney's 31st Regiment of Foot; The First Regiment Raised in the County of Cumberland in the Revolutionary War." *Collections and Proceedings of the Maine Historical Society*, 2d ser. 7:85-102, 151-85.

139. Gould, Edward Kalloch. *British and Tory Marauders on the Penobscot.* Rockland, Me., 1932.

A list of men in the "coast guard" companies of Knox County, Maine. Name and rank only.

140. Gratz, Simon. "The Generals of the Continental Line in the Revolutionary War." *Pennsylvania Magazine of History and Biography* 27 (1903):385-403.

Corrects other lists which excluded generals by brevet. Promotion records.

141. "The Green Mountain Boys; and Men with Ethan Allen at Ticonderoga." *Vermont Antiquarian* 3 (1904-5):138-43.

Four separate lists: revolutionary soldiers of Newbury, Vt., approximately 55 entries (names only); revolutionary soldiers of Lebanon, N.H., approximately 40 names with data from gravestone inscriptions; Green Mountain boys, approximately 250 names with rank; men with Ethan Allen at Ticonderoga, approximately 90 entries (names only).

142. Gwathmey, John Hastings. *Historical Register of Virginians in the Revolution: Soldiers, Sailors, Marines; 1775-1783.* Richmond: Deitz Press, 1938. Reprint ed., Baltimore: Genealogical Publishing Co., 1973.

Approximately 64,500 names in alphabetical order with very brief military service data. Source citations. An important list, incorporating Eckenrode's earlier work (*see* 240).

143. Hamersly, Thomas H. S., ed. *Complete General Navy Register of the United States, from 1776-1887 . . . Containing the Names of All the Officers of the Navy, Volunteer and Regular . . . 1776-1887.* New York, 1888.

144. ———. *Complete Regular Army Register of the United States (1778-1879), Together with . . . Various Tables.* Washington, D.C., 1880.

Lists of officers for 1779-80 by military organization, thereunder by rank and date of commission. Approximately 2,500 names.

145. Hanson, Willis Tracy, Jr. *A History of Schenectady during the Revolution [with] . . . Individual Records of the Inhabitants during That Period.* Brattleboro, Vt.: privately printed, 1916.

Short biographical sketches of soldiers and civilians.

146. *Hartland [Conn.] Patriotic Celebration.* Winsted, Conn.: H. B. Case, 1930.

List of 356 men who served in the Revolution.

147. Headley, J. T. *The Chaplains and Clergy of the Revolution.* New York, 1864.

Approximately forty full biographical sketches, many of prominent figures.

148. Heaton, Ronald E. *Masonic Membership of the General Officers of the Continental Army.* Washington, D.C.: Masonic Service Assoc., 1965.

149. Heitman, Francis B. *Historical Register of Officers of the Continental Army during the War of the Revolution, April, 1775 to December, 1783.* 2d rev. ed. Washington, D.C.: Rare Book Shop Publishing Co., 1914. Reprint ed., Baltimore: Genealogical Publishing Co., 1969.
Extensive military service records of approximately 14,000 officers. The most important compilation of officers.

150. Hillard, Elias Brewster. *The Last Men of the Revolution: A Photograph of Each from Life ... Accompanied by Brief Biographical Sketches.* Hartford: N. A. & R. A. Moore, 1864. 2d ed. Barre, Mass.: Barre Publishers, 1968.
Biographical sketches of six men, with photographs.

151. Hoenstein, Floyd G. *Military Services and Genealogical Records of Soldiers of Blair County, Pennsylvania.* Hallidaysburg, Pa.: Telegraph Press, 1940.
Approximately 135 sketches of soldiers ranging from a very brief statement on military service to extensive entries containing biographical and military service data.

152. House, Charles J., comp. *Names of Soldiers of the American Revolution Who Applied for State Bounty under Resolves of March 17, 1835, March 24, 1836, and March 20, 1838, as Appears of Record in Land Office.* Augusta, Me., 1893. Reprint ed., Baltimore: Genealogical Publishing Co., 1967.
List of 980 names compiled from Maine pension and bounty land records. Limited military service data and some genealogical information. Approximately one-half of the applications represented by names on this list were filed by widows.

153. Houts, Alice Kenyoun (Mrs. Hale), comp. "Revolutionary Soldiers Buried in Missouri." Reproduced typescript. 1966. DLC.
Approximately 850 biographical sketches in alphabetical order. Entries vary widely; many contain vital statistics and extensive genealogical data. Source citations.

154. Howe, Archibald Murray. *Colonel John Brown of Pittsfield, Massachusetts: The Brave Accuser of Benedict Arnold.* Boston: W. B. Clarke & Co., 1908.
List of approximately 400 names with rank only.

155. Howe, Octavius T. "Beverly Privateers in the American Revolution." *Publications of the Colonial Society of Massachusetts* 1 (1892): 318–435.

Includes a list of privateering vessels. Some entries give names of individuals. Appendix is a list of approximately 150 officers with residence, rank, vessel, and date of commission.

156. Illinois Adjutant General's Office. *Roll of Honor: Record of Burial Places of Soldiers, Sailors, Marines, and Army Nurses of All Wars of the United States Buried in Illinois.* 2 vols. Springfield, 1929.

Revolutionary soldiers appear infrequently among soldiers from other wars. Entry gives military organization, date of death, and place of interment.

157. Illinois State Genealogical Society. *Soldiers of the American Revolution Buried in Illinois.* Compiled by Mrs. John S. Devanny. Springfield, 1975.

Full biographical sketches with vital statistics, military service data, and genealogical information for approximately 1,000 soldiers. Source citations.

158. Johnson, Amandus. *Swedish Contributions to American Freedom, 1776–1783; Including a Sketch of the Background of the Revolution, Together with an Account of the Engagements in Which Swedish Officers Participated, and Biographical Sketches of These Men.* 2 vols. Philadelphia: Swedish Colonial Foundation, 1953–57.

Approximately seventy biographical sketches. Content varies. Most of these men fought with the French.

159. Johnston, Henry Phelps. *Yale and Her Honor-Roll in the American Revolution, 1775–1783; Including Original Letters, Record of Service, and Biographical Sketches.* New York, 1888.

Full biographical sketches for approximately 200 men, mostly high-ranking officers, surgeons, or chaplains. Military service data emphasized, but vital statistics and other biographical information included.

160. Johnston, Ross B. *West Virginia in the American Revolution. Publications of the West Virginia Historical Society,* no. 1. Parkersburg: West Augusta Historical and Genealogical Society, 1959.

Over 1,300 biographical sketches of soldiers from present-day West Virginia. Entries vary from gravestone inscriptions to full pension abstracts.

161. Kaminkow, Marion, and Kaminkow, Jack, eds. and comps. *Mariners of the American Revolution.* Baltimore: Magna Carta Book Co., 1967.

List of approximately 4,000 men, mostly privateers who were captured on the seas, with a brief statement on their capture.

162. Kidder, Frederic. *History of the First New Hampshire Regiment in the War of the Revolution.* Albany, 1868. Reprint ed., Hampton, N.H.: P. E. Randall, 1973.

   Contains a collection of rolls.

163. ————. *Military Operations in Eastern Maine and Nova Scotia during the Revolution, Chiefly Compiled from the Journals and Letters of Colonel John Allan.* Albany, 1867.

   Includes rolls of Indians in United States service.

164. King, J. Estelle Stewart, comp. "Mississippi Court Records, 1799–1835." Mimeographed. Beverly Hills, Calif., 1936. Reprint ed., Baltimore: Genealogical Publishing Co., 1969.

   Contains two short lists of pensioners in Tennessee and Mississippi. Limited military service and pension data for approximately seventy men.

165. Knight, Lucian Lamar, comp. *Georgia's Roster of the Revolution, Containing a List of the State's Defenders; Officers and Men; Soldiers and Sailors; Partisans and Regulars; Whether Enlisted from Georgia or Settled in Georgia after the Close of Hostilities; Compiled from Various Sources Including Official Documents, Both State and Federal, Certificates of Service, Land Grants, Pension Rolls and Other Records.* Atlanta: Index Printing Co., 1920. Reprint ed., Baltimore: Genealogical Publishing Co., 1967.

166. Lasseray, André. *Les Français sous les treize étoiles.* 2 vols. Mâcon: Protat Frères, 1935.

   Approximately 400 biographical sketches of French officers. Military service data emphasized, but vital statistics occasionally included. Source citations.

167. Lazenby, Mary E., comp. *Catawba Frontier, 1775–1781: Memories of Pensioners.* Washington, D.C.: privately printed, 1950.

   Pension abstracts for approximately 100 men.

168. Lewis, Virgil A. "The Soldiery of West Virginia in the French and Indian War, Lord Dunmore's War, the Revolution . . . the War with Mexico." *3rd Biennial Report of the State [West Virginia] Department of Archives and History*, pp. 39–118. Charleston: News-Mail Co., 1910. Reprint ed., Baltimore: Genealogical Publishing Co., 1972.

   Primarily lists of pensioners extracted from published lists.

169. Linn, John Blair, and Egle, William H., eds. *Pennsylvania in the*

War of the Revolution, Battalions and Line, 1775-1783. Pennsylvania Archives, 2d ser., vols. 10, 11. Harrisburg, 1880.

Contains extensive rolls, often with date of enlistment and casualty information.

170. "List of French Officers Who Served in the American Armies with Commissions from Congress Prior to the Treaties Made between France and the Thirteen United States of America." *Magazine of American History* 3 (1879):364-69.

Sixty-one French officers by date of commission with limited military service data.

171. "List of Officers in the Three Continental Battalions Raised in New Hampshire in 1776." *Collections, Topographical, Historical & Biographical Relating Principally to New Hampshire* 1 (1822): 123-26.

Approximately 120 officers by military unit with rank and residence.

172. "List of Officers, Sailors, and Marines of the Virginia Navy in the American Revolution." *Virginia Magazine of History and Biography* 1 (1894):64-75.

Approximately 600 names by rank and service.

173. McAllister, Joseph Thompson. *Index to Saffell's List of Virginia Soldiers in the Revolution.* Hot Springs, Va.: McAllister Publishing Co., 1913.

A partial index to *Saffell's List* (*see* 213) plus index of Virginia officers in *Calendar of Virginia State Papers* (*see* 20).

174. ———. *Virginia Militia in the Revolutionary War; McAllister's Data.* Hot Springs, Va.: McAllister Publishing Co., 1913.

Various lists of Virginia militia taken primarily from published pension lists. One section contains 250 brief pension abstracts. Name index contains approximately 2,800 entries.

175. McCall, Mrs. Ettie (Tidwell). *Roster of Revolutionary Soldiers in Georgia.* 3 vols. Vol. 1, Atlanta: Daughters of the American Revolution, Georgia, 1941. Reprint ed., Baltimore: Genealogical Publishing Co., 1968. Vols. 2 and 3, Baltimore: Genealogical Publishing Co., 1968-69.

A large and varied work which contains vital statistics, extensive genealogical and limited military service data for soldiers who had some association with the state of Georgia. Also includes previously published lists. Accurate estimate of the number of soldiers included is impossible. Volume 3 provides a comprehensive index to names in all three volumes.

176. McClellan, Edwin N. "Marine Officers of the Revolution."
     Daughters of the American Revolution Magazine 66 (1932):560-68.

177. McGhee, Lucy Kate, comp. "Missouri Revolutionary Soldiers,
     War of 1812 and Indian Wars—Pension List." Reproduced type-
     script. Washington, D.C., [1955?]. Vi, and other repositories.

     McGhee has compiled a number of unpublished items such as this
     one. A full list is contained in the *National Union Catalog.*

178. McSherry, James. *A History of Maryland from Its Settlement in
     1634 to the Year 1848.* Baltimore, 1850.

     Appendixes contain various lists of Maryland officers.

179. MacWethy, L. D. *Col. Jacob Klock's Regiment: Second Tryon
     County Militia in the Revolution.* St. Johnsville, N.Y.: Enterprise &
     News, 1930.

     List of approximately 1,200 names with rank and some very limited
     military service data.

180. Maginnis, Thomas H., Jr. *The Irish Contribution to America's
     Independence.* Philadelphia: Doire Publishing Co., 1913.

     A list of approximately 1,000 men with Irish surnames by regiment
     and rank. Some additional information on high-ranking officers.

181. Massachusetts, Secretary of the Commonwealth. *Massachusetts
     Soldiers and Sailors of the Revolutionary War: A Compilation from
     the Archives.* 17 vols. Boston, 1896-1908.

     Service records compiled from the large body of documents in the
     State House, Boston. Approximately 180,000 entries, but duplica-
     tion is evident. An invaluable compilation.

182. Mather, Frederic Gregory. *The Refugees of 1776 from Long
     Island to Connecticut.* Albany: J. B. Lyon Co., 1913.

     Approximately 1,300 biographical sketches with vital statistics,
     genealogical information, and military service data where appli-
     cable. Other lists include one of approximately 400 Long Island
     refugees serving in Connecticut forces with brief military service
     data.

183. Maurer, Jean. *Berks County Revolutionary Soldiers; Contained in
     Penna. Archives, 3rd Series, Volume VI; Penna. Archives, 5th
     Series, Volume V; National Geneological* [sic] *Quarterly, Volume
     XII, No. 1, March 1923; American Historical Register, Volume 2,
     Page 1457-1469; American Historical Register, Volume 3, Page 43-
     64; History of Hain's Church, Page 56-57; Forces American Archives,
     5th Series, Volume 1, Page 962-963.* N.p., 19-.

184. Mell, Annie R. "Revolutionary Soldiers Buried in Alabama." *Transactions of the Alabama Historical Society* 4 (1899-1903): 527-72.

Sketches of approximately thirty-five soldiers. Content varies. Most contain vital statistics. Longer entries contain genealogical and extensive military service data.

185. Metcalf, Bryce. *Original Members and Other Officers Eligible to the Society of the Cincinnati, 1783-1938; with ... Lists of the Officers of the General and State Societies.* Strasburg, Va.: Shenandoah Publishing House, 1938.

186. Middlebrook, Louis Frank. *History of Maritime Connecticut during the American Revolution, 1775-1783.* 2 vols. Salem, Mass.: Essex Institute, 1925.

Crew lists for ships of the Connecticut navy.

187. Miller, Florence Hazen. *Memorial Album of Revolutionary Soldiers, 1776.* Crete, Nebr., 1958.

Full biographical sketches for 380 men. Selection dictated by the existence of pictures or portraits of the men. Mostly officers.

188. Miller, Frank Burton. *Soldiers and Sailors of the Plantation of Lower St. Georges, Maine, Who Served in the War for American Independence.* Rockland, Me., 1931.

Biographical sketches for approximately 100 men. Military service data and vital statistics. Some very extensive entries.

189. Montgomery, Morton L. *History of Berks County, Pennsylvania, in the Revolution, from 1774 to 1783.* Reading, Pa., 1894.

Extensive lists of men, many with German surnames. Biographical sketches for approximately seventy men, mostly officers.

190. Murray, Thomas Hamilton. *Irish Rhode Islanders in the American Revolution with Some Mention of Those Serving in the Regiments of Elliott, Lippitt, Topham, Crary, Angell, Olney, Greene, and Other Noted Commanders.* Providence: American-Irish Historical Society, 1903.

Lists of individuals with Irish surnames. Limited military service data. Name index has approximately 700 entries, not all of which are Irish.

191. Nell, William C. *The Colored Patriots of the American Revolution, with Sketches of Several Distinguished Colored Persons: To Which Is Added a Brief Survey of the Condition and Prospects of Colored Americans.* Boston, 1855.

Some biographical mention of "Colored Patriots." Not all of the

black men and women treated in this work saw military service nor
are all the accounts confined to the revolutionary period.

192. Newman, Debra L., comp. *List of Black Servicemen Compiled
from the War Department Collection of Revolutionary War Records.*
National Archives Special List no. 36. Washington, D.C.: National
Archives, 1974.

Three separate lists of black soldiers extracted from *Index to Compiled Service Records* (*see* 4, 5), *Numbered Record Books* (*see* 19),
and *Special Index to Numbered Records* (*see* 30), all in the National Archives. The lists contain approximately 1,100 names, with
some duplication, and give state, rank, and military unit. Citations allow these lists to be used as an index.

193. Newman, Harry Wright. *Maryland Revolutionary Records; Data
Obtained from 3,050 Pension Claims and Bounty Land Applications,
Including 1,000 Marriages of Maryland Soldiers and a List of 1,200
Proved Services of Soldiers and Patriots of Other States.* Washington,
D.C.: privately printed, 1938. Reprint ed., Baltimore: Genealogical
Publishing Co., 1967.

List of pensioners with date of birth, rank, and military organization. List of bounty land recipients with rank and data on land
grant. List of nonpensioned Maryland soldiers found in pension
applications with rank and military organization. List of non-
Maryland soldiers found in pension applications with state of
service. List of marriages established by pension applications with
names of bride and groom, date and place of marriage. Number of
names probably in excess of 3,000.

194. New York State Committee of Historical Research and Preserva-
tions. "Grave Records of Revolutionary Soldiers Buried in New
York." 11 vols. Mimeographed. New York, 1938. DNDAR.

Brief biographical data in some entries, name only in others.

195. New York (State) Comptroller's Office. *New York in the Revolution as Colony and State.* 2 vols. Albany: J. B. Lyon Co., 1901–4.

Volume 1 is a list of approximately 50,000 men from New York
who performed military service. Alphabetical arrangement by
military organization with rank. Volume 2 is a collection of documents with some scattered lists of names.

196. New York (State) University, Executive Committee of the One
Hundred and Fiftieth Anniversary of the American Revolution.
Souvenir Program: One Hundred Fiftieth Anniversary of the Battle

of Oriskany and the Siege and Relief of Fort Stanwix. Albany: J. B. Lyon Co., 1927.

> Approximately 475 names with very brief military service data.

197. Noailles, Amblard Marie Raymond Amedié, Vicomte de. *Marins et soldats français en Amérique pendant la guerre de l'Indépendance des États-Unis (1778-1783).* Paris: Perrin & Co., 1903.

> Appendixes contain lists of officers by naval vessel and military unit with rank only.

198. O'Brien, Michael Joseph. *A Hidden Phase of American History: Ireland's Part in America's Struggle for Liberty.* New York: Dodd, Mead, and Co., 1919. Reprint ed., Baltimore: Genealogical Publishing Co., 1973.

> Lists of men with Irish surnames. Limited military service data.

199. ———. *The Irish at Bunker Hill: Evidence of Irish Participation in the Battle of 17 June 1775.* Edited by Catherine Sullivan. Shannon: Irish University Press, 1968.

> Military service and biographical data, extensive at times, for men with Irish surnames.

200. Ohio Adjutant General's Office and Daugthers of the American Revolution, Ohio. *Official Roster of Soldiers of the American Revolution Buried in Ohio.* 3 vols. Columbus: F. J. Heer Printing Co., 1929-59.

> Biographical sketches of varying lengths. Content varies. Many entries contain vital statistics, genealogical information, and limited military service data. Volume 1 has approximately 3,500 names. Many names duplicated in volumes 2 and 3.

201. *The Patriots of the Revolution of '76: Sketches of the Survivors.* Boston, 1864.

> Biographical sketches for twenty-three men still on the pension rolls at the time of the Civil War. Vital statistics and military service data.

202. Paullin, Charles Oscar. *The Navy of the American Revolution: Its Administration, Its Policy, and Its Achievements.* Chicago: Burrows Brothers Co., 1906.

> Lists of vessels and officers.

203. Peterson, Clarence Stewart. "Known Military Dead during the Revolutionary War." Mimeographed. Baltimore, 1959. Reprint ed., Baltimore: Genealogical Publishing Co., 1967.

> Approximately 9,500 names. Notation indicates whether men were

killed in action or died from other causes. Military organization, date of, and occasionally place of, death.

204. Potter, Chandler E. *The Military History of the State of New Hampshire from Its Settlement, in 1623 to the Rebellion in 1861.* 2 vols. *New Hampshire Adjutant General's Report.* Concord, 1866, 1868. Reprint ed., with added indexes, Baltimore: Genealogical Publishing Co., 1972.

Scattered muster rolls and biographical sketches of officers.

205. Powell, William H., comp. *List of Officers of the Army of the United States from 1779 to 1900.* New York: L. R. Hamersly & Co., 1900.

Approximately 1,000 names of revolutionary officers with military organization and date of commission.

206. Pruitt, Jayne Conway Garlington. *Revolutionary War Pension Applicants Who Served from South Carolina.* Fairfax County, Va., 1946.

207. Quisenberry, Anderson Chenault, comp. "Revolutionary Soldiers in Kentucky." In Sons of the American Revolution, Kentucky Society, *Yearbook.* 1896. Reprint ed., Baltimore: Genealogical Publishing Co., 1974.

Three separate lists: bounty land recipients, approximately 1,500 names with rank only; officers, sailors, and marines of the Virginia navy, approximately 600 names with rank only; Kentucky pensioners, approximately 3,000 names with rank, military organization, date of pension, and county of residence and age when pensioned.

208. Reade, Philip Hildreth. *Dedication Exercises at the Massachusetts Military Monument, Valley Forge, Pa.; ... Also, List of Officers in Massachusetts Organizations ... Who Served at Valley Forge.* Boston: Wright & Potter Printing Co., 1912.

Lists containing approximately 1,000 names. Limited military service data.

209. "Revolutionary Soldiers in Alabama." *Alabama Historical Quarterly* 6 (1944):523-686. Reprint ed., Tuscaloosa: Willo Publishing Co., 1959.

Approximately 750 entries varying widely in content. Data range from gravestone inscriptions to biographical sketches with vital statistics and military service data. Source citations.

210. Richards, Henry. "The Pennsylvania-German in the Revolutionary War, 1775-1783." *Proceedings of the Pennsylvania-German Society,* vol. 17, 1906.

Includes rolls, lists, and biographical sketches.

211. Richardson, Marian M., and Mize, Jessie J., comps. *1832 Cherokee Land Lottery: Index to Revolutionary Soldiers, Their Widows and Orphans Who Were Fortunate Drawers*. Danielsville, Ga.: Heritage Papers, 1969.

Alphabetical list of 742 revolutionary war soldiers, widows, and orphans with the lot number they drew and place of residence. Approximately 40 percent are widows. Index to James F. Smith, *Cherokee Land Lottery* (*see* 27).

212. Rider, Sidney Smith. *An Historical Inquiry Concerning the Attempt to Raise a Regiment of Slaves by Rhode Island during the War of the Revolution*. Providence, 1880.

Contains a list from state treasury records of slaves enlisted into Rhode Island Continental regiments.

213. Saffell, William T. R. *Records of the Revolutionary War Containing the Military and Financial Correspondence of Distinguished Officers; Names of the Officers and Privates of Regiments, Companies, and Corps . . . a List of Distinguished Prisoners of War . . . .* Baltimore: C. C. Saffell, 1894. Partly indexed in Joseph Thompson McAllister, *Index to Saffell's List of Virginia Soldiers in the Revolution* (Hot Springs, Va.: McAllister Publishing Co., 1913). Reprint ed., Baltimore: Genealogical Publishing Co., 1969.

Extensive lists of names in a variety of military units with limited military service data including length of enlistment. Includes other lists, for example, prisoners released or exchanged.

214. Sanderson, Howard Kendall. *Lynn [Mass.] in the Revolution*. 2 vols. Boston: W. B. Clarke Co., 1909.

Approximately 550 full biographical sketches with vital statistics, genealogical information, military service data, and facsimile signatures.

215. Schenck, David. *North Carolina, 1780-81; Being a History of the Invasion of the Carolinas by the British Army under Lord Cornwallis in 1780-81*. Raleigh, 1889.

Appendix contains list of approximately 975 officers with date of commission in North Carolina Continentals. Alphabetical by rank.

216. Seay, Elizabeth Slater. *Alabama Bound Revolutionary War Patriots in Jefferson County*. Reproduced typescript. Montgomery: Goodway Copy Centers, 1971.

Approximately thirty names of soldiers, principally pensioners, with brief and varied information. Data on migration of seventeen men.

217. Slager, A. L. "Revolutionary War Soldiers Buried in Clark County, Ohio." *Ohio Archaeological and Historical Quarterly* 37 (1928):86–100.

   List of thirty-seven names with place of interment. Second list gives additional data on twenty-five of these. Content varies. Most entries contain vital statistics, some have extensive military service and biographical data.

218. Smith, Charles R. *Marines in the Revolution: A History of the Continental Marines in the American Revolution, 1775–1783.* Washington, D.C.: History and Museums Division, United States Marine Corps, 1975.

   Biographical sketches of approximately 120 Marine officers. Most contain vital statistics, extensive military service data, and other biographical material. Work contains much additional information on the Marines.

219. Smith, Jonathan. *Peterborough, New Hampshire, in the American Revolution.* Peterborough: Peterborough Historical Society, 1913.

   Approximately 225 detailed biographical sketches of soldiers. Vital statistics, military service data, and other biographical material. Source citations.

220. Smith, Susan A., comp. *Muster Rolls of Pembroke, Massachusetts, during the Revolution, Taken from State Archives, Followed by an Alphabetical List of Soldiers.* N.p., 1912.

   Approximately 500 names with rank for commissioned and non-commissioned officers. Infrequent notation such as "transient" or "Indian."

221. Society of Old Brooklynites, Brooklyn, New York. *A Christmas Reminder, Being the Names of about Eight Thousand Persons, a Small Portion of the Number Confined on Board the British Prison Ships during the War of the Revolution.* Brooklyn, 1888.

   List of approximately 8,000 men incarcerated on the prison ship *Jersey.*

222. Society of the Cincinnati, Massachusetts. *Memorials of the Massachusetts Society of the Cincinnati.* Boston, 1873, 1890, 1931, 1964.

   Full biographical sketches of members, including descendants. Alphabetical by surname of original member. Sketches of revolutionary officers include vital statistics, extensive military service data, genealogical information, and other biographical material. The 1964 edition concentrated on expanding the sketches of lesser-known original members, and the longer sketches of prominent figures in the earlier editions were shortened.

223. Sons of the American Revolution. *A National Register of the Society Sons of the American Revolution.* 2 vols. New York: A. H. Kellogg, 1902.

Similar to the DAR *Lineage Books* (*see* 84), but with less information on the individual soldier and a greater attention to members.

224. Sons of the American Revolution, Connecticut; General David Humphreys Branch Number One. *Revolutionary Characters of New Haven; ... also, List of Men so Far as They are Known from the Territory Embraced in the Town of New Haven, Connecticut, Who Served in the Continental Army and Militia and on Continental and State Vessels and Privateers, and Those Who Rendered Other Patriotic Services during the War of the Revolution, and a Record of Known Casualties; Together with the Location of Known Graves in and about New Haven of Patriots of 1775-1783 and Catalogue of the Officers and Members of Gen. David Humphreys Branch Since Its Organization.* New Haven, 1911.

Lists containing approximately 1,000 names. Sporadic casualty information. Also contains a grave list with approximately 175 names.

225. ———. "Roster of Graves and Monuments to Patriots of 1775-1783 in and Adjacent to New Haven County." Reproduced typescript. New Haven: SAR, 1933. DLC.

List of 1,050 names with limited service data, place of burial, and infrequent instances of vital statistics.

226. Sons of the American Revolution, Maine. *Maine at Valley Forge: Proceedings at the Unveiling of the Maine Marker, October 17, 1907; also Roll of Maine Men at Valley Forge.* 2d ed. Augusta: Burleigh & Flint, 1910.

List of approximately 1,000 names with place of residence.

227. Sons of the American Revolution, Massachusetts; Old Middlesex Chapter, Lowell. *In Memoriam; Citizen Soldiers of Dracut, Mass., Who Served in the War of the American Revolution, 1775-1783.* Lowell [?], 1905[?].

228. Sons of the American Revolution, Ohio. "Revolutionary Soldiers Buried in Ohio." Sons of the American Revolution, Ohio Society, *Yearbook*, 1898, pp. 162-214; 1900, pp. 89-94.

229. Sons of the Revolution, Kentucky. *Yearbook of the Society, Sons of the Revolution, in the Commonwealth of Kentucky, 1894-1913*

and Catalogue of Military Land Warrants Granted by the Common-
wealth of Virginia to Soldiers and Sailors of the Revolution. Compiled
by Samuel M. Wilson. Lexington, 1913. Reprint ed., *Catalogue of*
Revolutionary Soldiers and Sailors of the Commonwealth of Virginia
to Whom Land Bounty Warrants Were Granted by Virginia for Mili-
tary Services in the War for Independence. Baltimore: Genealogical
Publishing Co., 1967.

    List of approximately 3,650 soldiers and sailors with limited mili-
tary service data. *Yearbook* also includes a list of approximately
1,200 members of the Cincinnati, by state with rank.

230. Stamford [Conn.] Genealogical Society. "Revolutionary Soldier
Review." *Bulletin of the Stamford Genealogical Society,* 1961-.

    Alphabetical list of Connecticut soldiers.

231. Stevens, John Austin. "The French in Rhode Island." *Magazine of*
American History 3 (1879):385–436.

    Contains a list showing the location of the quarters of individual
French officers. The name of the owner of the house is given.

232. Steuart, Reiman. *A History of the Maryland Line in the Revolu-*
tionary War, 1775-1783. N.p., Society of the Cincinnati of Maryland,
1969.

    Detailed information on the Maryland officer corps. Biographical
sketches emphasizing military service data which is often extensive;
vital statistics frequently included.

233. Stewart, Robert Armistead. *The History of Virginia's Navy of the*
Revolution. Richmond: Mitchell & Hotchkiss, 1934.

    Includes a list of approximately 2,000 names with limited military
service data. Source citations.

234. Stryker, William Scudder. *General Maxwell's Brigade of the New*
Jersey Continental Line in the Expedition against the Indians, in the
Year 1779. Trenton, 1885.

    Contains a complete roster for the brigade during the expedition.
Name, and rank by company.

235. ———. *New Jersey Continental Line in the Virginia Campaign of*
1781. Trenton, 1882.

    Roster of New Jersey troops. Approximately 900 names by com-
pany with rank.

236. Stryker, William Scudder, comp. *Official Register of the Officers*
and Men of New Jersey in the Revolutionary War. Trenton, 1872.
Also, James W. S. Campbell, *Digest and Revision of Stryker's Officers*
and Men of New Jersey ... (New York: Williams Printing Co., 1911

[*see* 64]). Reprinted., Baltimore: Genealogical Publishing Co., 1967. Also, New Jersey Historical Records Survey Program, *Index of the Official Register of the Officers and Men of New Jersey . . .* (Newark: Historical Records Survey, 1941). Reprint ed., Baltimore: Genealogical Publishing Co., 1965.

> Extensive lists of names compiled from New Jersey documents. Divided into two sections, one for Continentals, the other for state troops and militia, thereunder by rank in alphabetical order. Limited military service data for officers. Military organization only for privates or, for militia, county from which served. Separately compiled index has over 14,000 name entries.

237. Summers, Lewis Preston. *Annals of Southwest Virginia, 1769–1800.* Abingdon, Va.: privately printed, 1929. Reprint ed., Baltimore: Genealogical Publishing Co., 1970.

> Major list of approximately 1,900 names of soldiers from southwest Virginia, with military service data. Other smaller lists. Also includes county court records for five counties in southwest Virginia.

238. Thompson, Lucien, comp. *Revolutionary Pension Declarations, Strafford County, 1820–1832, Comprising Sketches of Soldiers of the Revolution, Compiled from the Court Records.* Manchester, N.H.: Ruemely Press, 1907.

> Pension abstracts from court records.

239. Tucker, Charles C., comp. *A List of Pensioners in the State of Massachusetts, Comprising Invalid Pensioners, and Revolutionary Pensioners under the Acts of Congress Passed March 18, 1818, May 15, 1828, and June 7, 1832.* Washington, D.C., 1854.

> List of approximately 3,800 names arranged by applicable pension act, thereunder by place of residence. No further information.

240. Virginia State Library, Department of Archives and History. *List of Revolutionary Soldiers of Virginia.* Compiled by H. J. Eckenrode. Special Report for 1911. Supplement, Special Report for 1912. Richmond: D. Bottom, 1912, 1913.

> Alphabetical list of approximately 35,000 names. Includes very brief military service data for Continental, state, militia, and naval forces. Source citations. Supplement contains approximately 8,500 additional names. (*See also* 142.)

241. "Vital Statistics Copied from *The Maine Farmer*, 1833–1852." 3 vols. Typescript. *American Periodicals 1800–1850.* Ann Arbor: University Microfilms, 1949–.

The third volume is a compiled list of death notices. A separate section of this volume lists those men who had served in the Revolution, with age and residence at death and date of death. Infrequent instances of limited military service data. Genealogical information may be obtained by consulting the main list of death notices, which is in alphabetical order by surname.

242. Walker, Mrs. Harriet J. *Revolutionary Soldiers Buried in Illinois.* Los Angeles: Standard Printing Co., 1917. Reprint ed., Baltimore: Genealogical Publishing Co., 1967.

Approximately 700 biographical sketches. Limited military service data and some information on westward migration.

243. Waters, Margaret R. *Revolutionary Soldiers Buried in Indiana: 300 Names Not Listed in the "Roster of Soldiers and Patriots of the American Revolution Buried in Indiana."* Indianapolis, 1949. Reprint ed., Baltimore: Genealogical Publishing Co., 1970.

Vital statistics, genealogical information, and limited military service data for soldiers not included in DAR, Indiana, *Roster of Soldiers and Patriots Buried in Indiana* (*see* 90). Source citations.

244. ———. *Revolutionary Soldiers Buried in Indiana: A Supplement; 485 Names Not Listed in the "Roster of Soldiers and Patriots of the American Revolution Buried in Indiana"* (*1938*); nor in *"Revolutionary Soldiers Buried in Indiana"* (*1949*). Indianapolis, 1954.

Additional entries with vital statistics, military service data, and extensive genealogical data. Source citations. Includes other lists of, for example, widows who lived in Indiana whose husbands died in other states. Also contains additions and corrections to 1949 compilation. A first-rate example of this type of work.

245. White, David Oliver. *Connecticut's Black Soldiers, 1775–1783.* Connecticut Bicentennial Series, no. 4. Chester: Pequot Press, 1973.

Appendix contains a list of 289 black soldiers with town from which they served, dates of service, and whether pensioned. No index.

246. White, Katherine Keogh. *The King's Mountain Men: The Story of the Battle, with Sketches of the American Soldiers Who Took Part.* Dayton, Va.: J. K. Ruebush Co., 1924. Reprint ed., Baltimore: Genealogical Publishing Co., 1970.

Approximately 350 biographical sketches. Content varies. Military service data, genealogical information, and vital statistics.

247. Wild, Helen T. *Medford in the Revolution: Military History of Medford, Massachusetts, 1765–1783; also List of Soldiers and Civil Officers, with Genealogical and Biographical Notes.* Medford: J. C. Miller, 1903.

Approximately 300 names. Content of entries varies, some with only very limited military service data, others with vital statistics and genealogical data. Black soldiers are noted.

248. Wolf, Simon. *The American Jew as Patriot, Soldier, and Citizen.* Philadelphia and New York, 1895.

Brief statement of military service for forty-six men.

249. Womer, William Frederick. "Revolutionary Soldiers and Patriots of Lancaster County." *Papers Read before the Lancaster County Historical Society* 34 (1930):145–68.

Approximately 75 obituaries extracted from Lancaster newspapers. Information varies widely. This volume also contains a list of 164 soldiers buried in Lancaster County.

250. Wood, Sumner Gilbert, comp. *Soldiers and Sailors of the Revolution from Blandford, Massachusetts.* West Medway, Mass., 1933.

Various lists from original rolls. A descriptive roll of men enlisted for three years or the duration of the war is included. Index has approximately 510 name entries.

251. Wright, Albert Hazen. "The Sullivan Expedition of 1779: The Losses." New York Historical Studies. Reproduced typescript. N.p., 1965 [?]. DLC.

Lists of names by military organization with casualty information.

252. ——. "The Sullivan Expedition of 1779: The Regimental Rosters of Men." Reproduced typescript. Ithaca [?], N.Y., 1965. DLC.

Lists containing approximately 5,850 names by military organization with rank.

3

OTHER SOURCES OF
BIOGRAPHICAL INFORMATION

☆

The materials discussed and listed in the preceding chapters do not exhaust the resources for historical and genealogical research on the military personnel of the American Revolution. The purpose of this chapter is to direct researchers to further sources of information.

Primary sources were discussed in the first chapter and specific mention was made of important documents in the National Archives. Manuscript collections, however, exist throughout the country. The Henry E. Huntington Library in San Marino, California, for example, has a collection of revolutionary war orderly books. But the vast majority of documentary materials containing biographical information on soldiers and sailors is to be found within the boundaries of the original thirteen states. Large collections are held in state archives and historical societies as well as in university libraries. Smaller, yet often homogeneous, bodies of records may be found in county court houses and local historical societies.

A list of published guides, which will assist researchers in locating manuscript sources, follows.

253. Bell, Whitfield J., Jr., and Smith, Murphy D. *Guide to the Archives and Manuscript Collections of the American Philosophical Society. Memoirs of the American Philosophical Society*, vol. 66. Philadelphia, 1966.
254. Billington, Ray Allen. "Guides to American History Manuscript Collections in Libraries of the United States." *Mississippi Valley Historical Review* 38 (1951-52): 467-96.
255. Blosser, Susan Sokol, and Wilson, Clyde Norman, Jr. *The Southern Historical Collection: A Guide to Manuscripts*. Chapel Hill: University of North Carolina Library, 1970. Also, *The Southern Historical Collection: Supplementary Guide to Manuscripts, 1970-1975*. Chapel Hill: University of North Carolina Library, 1976.
256. Boston Public Library. *Manuscripts of the American Revolution in the Boston Public Library: A Descriptive Catalog*. Boston: G. K. Hall, 1968.

257. Breton, Arthur J. *A Guide to the Manuscript Collections of the New-York Historical Society.* 2 vols. Westport, Conn.: Greenwood Press, 1972.

258. *Catalogue of the Manuscripts in the Collection of the Virginia Historical Society.* Richmond: W. E. Jones, 1901.

259. Clark, Alexander P. *The Manuscript Collections of the Princeton University Library: An Introductory Survey.* Princeton: Princeton University Press, 1958.

260. Cox, Richard J. "A Checklist of Revolutionary War Manuscript Collections Accessioned and Catalogued since Publication of *The Manuscript Collections of the Maryland Historical Society* (1968)." *Maryland Historical Magazine* 71 (1976):252–63. See 283.

261. Crabtree, Beth G. *Guide to Private Manuscript Collections in the North Carolina State Archives.* Raleigh: North Carolina State Department of Archives and History, 1964.

262. Cuthbert, Norma B., comp. *American Manuscript Collections in the Huntington Library for the History of the Seventeenth and Eighteenth Centuries.* San Marino, Calif., 1941.

263. Greene, Evarts B., and Morris, Richard B. *A Guide to the Principal Sources for Early American History (1600–1800) in the City of New York.* 2d ed. New York: Columbia University Press, 1953.

264. Hamer, Philip M., ed. *A Guide to Archives and Manuscripts in the United States.* New Haven: Yale University Press, 1961.

265. Historical Records Survey. *Calendar of the New Jersey State Library Manuscript Collection.* Newark: Historical Records Survey, 1939.

266. ———. *Checklist of Historical Records Survey Publications.* Bibliography of Research Project Reports, Works Projects Administration Technical Series, no. 7. Washington, D.C., 1943. Reprint ed., Baltimore: Genealogical Publishing Co., 1969.

267. ———. *Guide to Depositories of Manuscript Collections in Massachusetts.* Boston: Historical Records Survey, 1939.

268. ———. *Guide to Depositories of Manuscript Collections in New York State (Exclusive of New York City).* Albany: Historical Records Survey, 1941.

269. ———. *Guide to Depositories of Manuscript Collections in North Carolina.* Raleigh: North Carolina Historical Commission, 1940.

270. ———. *Guide to Depositories of Manuscript Collections in the United States: New Hampshire.* Manchester, N.H.: Historical Records Survey, 1940.

271. ———. *Guide to Depositories of Manuscript Collections in the United States: New Jersey.* Newark: Historical Records Survey, 1941.

272. Historical Records Survey, Pennsylvania. *Guide to the Manuscript Collections of the Historical Society of Pennsylvania.* 2d ed. Philadelphia: Historical Society of Pennsylvania, 1949.

273. Lincoln, Charles Henry, comp. *Naval Records of the American Revolution.* Washington, D.C.: Government Printing Office, 1906.

274. McCormack, Helen G. "A Provisional Guide to the Manuscripts in the South Carolina Historical Society." *South Carolina Historical and Genealogical Magazine* 45 (1944):111 through 48 (1947):180.

275. McIlwaine, H. R. "The Revolutionary War Material in the Virginia State Library." *Magazine of History* 10 (1909):143-50.

276. Maine University, Department of History and Government. *A Reference List of Manuscripts Relating to the History of Maine.* University of Maine Studies, 2d ser., no. 45. Orono, Me.: University of Maine Press, 1938.

277. Maryland Hall of Records Commission. *Calendar of Maryland State Papers.* Annapolis, 1943-.

278. ———. *Catalogue of Archival Material. Publications of the Maryland Hall of Records Commission,* no. 2. Annapolis, 1942.

279. Massachusetts Historical Society. *Catalog of Manuscripts of the Massachusetts Historical Society.* 7 vols. Boston: G. K. Hall, 1969.

280. Moore, John Hammond. *Research Materials in South Carolina: A Guide.* Columbia: University of South Carolina Press, 1967.

281. New York Public Library. *Dictionary Catalog of the Manuscript Division.* 2 vols. Boston: G. K. Hall, 1967.

282. Peckham, Howard H., comp. *Guide to the Manuscript Collections in the William L. Clements Library.* Ann Arbor, 1942. 2d ed., compiled by William S. Ewing. Ann Arbor, 1953.

283. Pedley, Avril J. M., ed. *The Manuscript Collections of the Maryland Historical Society.* Baltimore: Maryland Historical Society, 1968. *See* 260.

284. Pennsylvania Historical and Museum Commission. *Catalogue of the Manuscript Collection of the Pennsylvania State Archives.* Harrisburg: Pennsylvania Historical and Museum Commission, 1976.

285. ———. *Preliminary Guide to the Research Materials of the Pennsylvania Historical and Museum Commission.* Harrisburg: Pennsylvania Historical and Museum Commission, 1959.

286. Ruttenber, E. M. *Catalogue of Manuscripts and Relics in Washington's Head-quarters.* Newburgh, N.Y., 1890.

287. Sellers, John R.; Gawalt, Gerard W.; Smith, Paul H.; and van Ee, Patricia Molen. *Manuscript Sources in the Library of Congress for Research on the American Revolution.* Washington, D.C.: Government Printing Office, 1975.
288. Shelley, Fred. *A Guide to the Manuscript Collection of the New Jersey Historical Society. Collections of the New Jersey Historical Society*, no. 11. Newark, 1957.
289. Smith, Alice E. *Guide to the Manuscripts of the Wisconsin Historical Society.* Madison: State Historical Society of Wisconsin, 1944. Supplements 1 and 2. Madison, 1957, 1966.
290. Smith, Clifford Neal, comp. and ed. *Federal Land Series: A Calendar of Archival Materials on the Land Patents Issued by the United States Government, with Subject, Tract, and Name Indexes.* Chicago: American Library Association, 1972–.
291. Smith, Herbert, comp. *A Guide to the Manuscript Collection of the Rutgers University Library.* New Brunswick, N.J.: Rutgers University Press, 1964.
292. Stewart, Bruce W., and Mayer, Hans. *A Guide to the Manuscript Collection, Morristown National Historical Park.* Morristown, N.J., 196-?
293. Tilley, Nannie M., and Goodwin, Norma Lee, comps. *Guide to Manuscript Collections in the Duke University Library.* Durham, N.C.: Duke University Press, 1947.
294. United States Library of Congress. *National Union Catalogue of Manuscript Collections.* Hamden, Conn.: Shoe String Press, 1959–.
295. United States National Archives and Records Service. *Guide to the National Archives of the United States.* Washington, D.C.: National Archives and Records Service, 1974.
296. Winsor, Justin. *Calendar of the Sparks Manuscripts in Harvard College Library.* Cambridge, Mass., 1889.

Libraries such as the Newberry Library in Chicago and the National Society of the Daughters of the American Revolution Library in Washington, D.C., as well as many public libraries have responded to the widespread interest in genealogical and family history research. These institutions, like manuscript repositories, are valuable places to search for biographical information on revolutionary war military personnel.

The value of these institutions is threefold. They hold extensive collections of the published sources listed in the first chapter plus many of the secondary compilations, which few but the very largest university libraries systematically acquire, and genealogical material does not circulate through interlibrary loan.

The second advantage of this type of institution is that their holdings are not, of course, limited to military materials. Census, marriage, birth, death, and transcribed family Bible records, among others, are all available to aid the historian and the genealogist in linking the soldier to the civilian society he was raised to defend or to his relatives within that society.

The third advantage is that such institutions are depositories for unpublished materials compiled by researchers. Card catalogs may be used to locate items unique to a particular library or which exist in only a few other institutions. The catalog of the Daughters of the American Revolution Library, for example, contains many entries like Ruth Willys Chapter's "An Annotated List of Soldiers Buried in the Cemeteries of Ancient Hartford," and Jesse B. Abbe's manuscript compilation "The Revolutionary Soldiers Connected with the Town of Enfield, Connecticut."

The largest body of genealogical material in the world has been collected by the Genealogical Society of the Church of Jesus Christ of Latter-day Saints in Salt Lake City, Utah. There are approximately 140,000 bound items, well over 800,000 rolls of microfilm,[1] and many public documents (land records, court records, probate records, etc). Because most of these documents are well indexed, they have long been heavily used by genealogists and can be of considerable value in tracing the lives of the revolutionary war generation. Records have been filmed from all over the world, but the film library is particularly strong for the eastern seaboard of the United States. Although manuscript records have been emphasized, the Mormon Genealogical Society has also filmed indexes and compilations from many other repositories. A system of branch libraries open to the general public makes these resources widely available. For a small handling fee, items needed by individual researchers are loaned to branch libraries by the central library in Salt Lake City.

The card catalog for this collection, which is on microfilm (entry 303), is periodically updated and is available throughout the country. Organized geographically by state and thereunder by county, it is an

1. For additional information see Larry R. Gerlach and Michael L. Nicholls, "The Morman Genealogical Society and Research Opportunities in Early American History," *William and Mary Quarterly*, 3d ser. 32 (1975):625-29.

invaluable finding aid to many manuscript collections, to published sources, and to both published and unpublished secondary works.

Interest in genealogy is reflected not only in research facilities, but also in a number of serial publications, indexes, and methodological treatises. A selected list of genealogical finding aids and bibliographies follows.

297. *The American Genealogist, Being a Catalogue of Family Histories; a Bibliography of American Genealogy; or, A List of the Title-pages of Books and Pamphlets on Family History, Published in America, from 1771 to Date.* 5th ed. Albany: Joel Munsell's Sons, 1900.

298. American Society of Genealogists. *Genealogical Research: Methods and Sources.* Vol. 1, edited by Milton Rubincam. Vol. 2, edited by Kenn Stryker-Rodda. Washington, D.C.: American Society of Genealogists, 1960, 1971.

299. Cappon, Lester J. *American Genealogical Periodicals: A Bibliography with a Chronological Finding-List.* New York: New York Public Library, 1964.

300. Colket, Meredith Bright, and Bridges, Frank E. *Guide to Genealogical Records in the National Archives.* Washington, D.C.: National Archives, 1964.

301. Daughters of the American Revolution Library. *Catalogue of Genealogical and Historical Works.* Washington, D.C.: DAR, 1940.

302. Doane, Gilbert H. *Searching for Your Ancestors: The How and Why of Genealogy.* 4th ed. Minneapolis: University of Minnesota Press, 1973.

303. Genealogical Society of the Church of Jesus Christ of Latter-day Saints. *Microfilmed Catalogue: United States and Canadian Collection.* Salt Lake City, 1973–74.

304. *Index to American Genealogies and to Genealogical Material Contained in All Works Such as Town Histories, County Histories, Local Histories, Historical Society Publications, Biographies, Historical Periodicals, and Kindred Works* 5th ed. rev. Albany: Joel Munsell's Sons, 1908. Reprint ed., Baltimore: Genealogical Publishing Co., 1967.

305. Jacobus, Donald Lines. *Index to Genealogical Publications.* 3 vols. New Haven: privately printed, 1932–53. Reprint ed., Baltimore: Genealogical Publishing Co., 1973.

306. Kirkham, E. Kay. "Some of the Military Records of America (before 1900): Their Use and Value in Genealogical and Historical Research." Typescript. Washington, D.C., 1963. ICN.

307. Rider, Fremont J., ed. *The American Genealogical Biographical Index to American Genealogical, Biographical, and Local History Materials.* Middletown, Conn., 1952–.
308. Stevenson, Noel C. *Search and Research: The Researcher's Handbook; a Guide to Official Records and Library Sources for Investigators, Historians, Genealogists, Lawyers, and Librarians.* 2d ed., rev. Salt Lake City: Deseret Book Co., 1969.

Genealogical research has traditionally been linked to local history. The second chapter listed only those local histories, such as Howard Sanderson's work on Lynn, Massachusetts, which deal specifically with the revolutionary period. There are, however, thousands of local histories covering longer periods which contain a chapter or chapters on the revolutionary era. These works often contain biographical information on soldiers and sailors, frequently within the context of other genealogical information. George L. Rockwell's *The History of Ridgefield, Connecticut* (Ridgefield: privately printed, 1927), for example, contains a list of Ridgefield men in the revolutionary war and approximately fifty pages of information about them. Furthermore, this local history also includes sixty-five pages of vital records for the town as a whole, and so it is possible easily to place the soldier within the context of his local society.

Another instance of this type of work is Henry Hobart Vail's *Pomfret, Vermont* (edited by Emma Chandler White, 2 vols. [Boston: Cockayne, 1930]). The first volume of this work contains a list of sixty-two men with limited military service data and, where applicable, a notation that the soldier received a pension. But the value of Vail's work rests not on this list with its limited information. The second volume contains approximately 20 pages of vital records and 175 pages of genealogies in which many of the soldiers listed in the first volume may be found. Whether one wishes to seek an individual ancestor or to determine the socioeconomic status of the revolutionary war soldier, local histories provide valuable data. Following is a list of guides and bibliographies designed to assist the researcher in locating local histories and other sources of information on military personnel within specific geographic areas.

309. Brigham, Clarence Saunders. *List of Books upon Rhode Island History.* Rhode Island Educational Circulars, Historical Series no. 1. Providence: Rhode Island State Dept. of Education, 1908.
310. Burr, Nelson R. *A Narrative and Descriptive Bibliography of New*

Jersey. New Jersey Historical Series, vol. 21. New York: D. Van Nostrand Co., 1964.

311. Easterby, James Herald. *Guide to the Study and Reading of South Carolina History: A General Classified Bibliography*. Columbia: The Historical Commission of South Carolina, 1950. Reprint ed., with additions, Spartanburg, S.C.: Reprint Co., 1975.

312. Flagg, Charles A., comp. *A Guide to Massachusetts Local History*. Salem, Mass.: Salem Press Co., 1907.

313. Gilman, M. D. *The Bibliography of Vermont*. Burlington: Free Press Assoc., 1897.

314. Hammond, Otis Grant. *Hammond's Check List of New Hampshire Local History*. Edited by Jack Hanrahan. Rev. ed. *Bibliographies of New Hampshire*. Somersworth: New Hampshire Publishing Co., 1971.

315. Haskell, John D., Jr., ed. *Massachusetts: A Bibliography of Its History*. Bibliographies of New England History, vol. 1. Boston: G. K. Hall, 1976.

316. Kaminkow, Marion J., ed. *United States Local Histories in the Library of Congress: A Bibliography*. 4 vols. Baltimore: Magna Carta Book Co., 1974. Supplement and index. Baltimore, 1976.

317. Klein, Milton M. *New York in the American Revolution: A Bibliography*. Albany: New York State American Revolution Bicentennial Commission, 1974.

318. Lefler, Hugh Talmage. *A Guide to the Study and Reading of North Carolina History*. Chapel Hill: University of North Carolina Press, 1955.

319. Passano, Eleanor Phillips. *An Index of the Source Records of Maryland: Genealogical, Biographical, Historical*. Baltimore: privately printed, 1940. Reprint ed., Baltimore: Genealogical Publishing Co., 1967.

320. Peterson, Clarence Stewart. *Consolidated Bibliography of County Histories in Fifty States*. Baltimore: privately printed, 1961. Reprint ed., Baltimore: Genealogical Publishing Co., 1973.

321. Reed, H. Clay, and Reed, Marion Bjornson, comps. *A Bibliography of Delaware through 1960*. Newark, Del.: University of Delaware Press, 1966.

322. Rowland, Arthur Ray. *A Bibliography of the Writings on Georgia History*. Hamden, Conn.: Archon Books, 1966.

323. Swem, Earl Gregg. "A Bibliography of Virginia." *Bulletin of the Virginia State Library* 8 (1915):35-767.

324. Thornton, Mary Lindsay. *A Bibliography of North Carolina*,

1589-1956. Chapel Hill: University of North Carolina Press, 1958.
325. Turnbull, Robert J. *Bibliography of South Carolina, 1563-1950.* 5 vols. Charlottesville: University of Virginia Press, 1956.
326. Virginia State Library. *Virginia Local History: A Bibliography.* Richmond: Virginia State Library, 1971.
327. Wilkinson, Norman B., comp. *Bibliography of Pennsylvania History.* Edited by S. K. Stevens and Donald H. Kent. 2d ed. Harrisburg: Pennsylvania Historical and Museum Commission, 1957.
328. Williamson, Joseph. *Bibliography of Maine.* 2 vols. Portland, Me.: Thurston, 1896.

The following list contains a few miscellaneous but nonetheless significant items which may direct researchers to additional sources of biographical information on soldiers and sailors of the American revolutionary war.

329. Baker, Mary Ellen. "Bibliography of Lists of New England Soldiers." *New England Historical and Genealogical Register* 64 (1910): 61-72, 128-35, 228-37, 327-36; 65 (1911):11-19, 151-60.
330. Flagg, C. A., and Waters, W. O. "Virginia's Soldiers in the Revolution: A Bibliography of Muster and Pay Rolls, Regimental Histories, etc." *Virginia Magazine of History and Biography* 19 (1911): 402-14; 20 (1912):52-68, 181-94, 267-81; 21 (1913):337-46; 22 (1914): 57-67, 177-86.
331. Griffin, Appleton P. C., comp. *List of Works Relating to the French Alliance in the American Revolution.* Washington, D.C.: Library of Congress, 1907.
332. Hale, Richard W., Jr., ed. *Guide to Photocopied Historical Materials in the United States and Canada.* Ithaca, N.Y.: Cornell University Press, 1961.
333. Jenkins, William Sumner, comp. *A Guide to the Microfilm Collection of Early State Records.* Edited by Lillian A. Hamrich. Washington, D.C.: Library of Congress Photoduplication Service, 1950. Supplement. Washington, D.C.: Library of Congress Photoduplication Service, 1951.
334. Neeser, Robert Wilden. *Statistical and Chronological History of the United States Navy, 1775-1907.* 2 vols. New York: Macmillan, 1909.
335. Smith, Myron J. *Navies in the American Revolution: A Bibliography.* Metuchen, N.Y.: Scarecrow Press, 1973.

336. Swem, Earl Gregg. *Virginia Historical Index*. 2 vols. Roanoke, Va.: Stone Printing and Manufacturing Co., 1934–36.

337. Tyson, Carolyn A., and Gill, Rowland P., comps. *An Annotated Bibliography of Marines in the American Revolution*. Washington, D.C.: Historical Division, United States Marine Corps, 1972.

4

DIARIES, JOURNALS, MEMOIRS, AND AUTOBIOGRAPHIES

☆

The American Revolution encouraged men to keep records of their daily experiences and to publish their reminiscences. These traditional sources of historical information provide an important picture of the American Revolution through the eyes and words of the men who bore arms.

Each entry in the following list contains the name of the author and, where known, his rank and the state from which he served. Assignment of rank was not always easy and in the end was somewhat subjective. The general rule followed was to give the rank at the time the diary was written or the highest rank obtained during the Revolution. For postwar memoirs and autobiographies, the highest rank obtained during the Revolution was used.

Many diaries have been published or reprinted several times, and for these, several citations have been given. The first citation in a multiple entry is either the first instance of publication or the first instance of publication of a diary in its entirety. Subsequent citations to extracts and reprints are given in footnote style. The inclusive dates for diaries and journals are supplied where they are not given in the title. Wherever possible, the location of the manuscript of a published diary is given in Library of Congress National Union Catalog symbols. The location is given for all diaries that exist only in manuscript, and a key to symbols is provided at the beginning of this book.

Many different sources were used to compile this list, but three require special mention. The most important list of early American diaries is William Mathews's *American Diaries: An Annotated Bibliography of American Diaries Written prior to the Year 1861* (Berkeley and Los Angeles: University of California Press, 1945). Mathews's full annotations and complete citations facilitated the task of locating diaries of many military participants. Of equal importance, though not so convenient because of the brevity of the annotations, is Mathews's *American Diaries in Manuscript, 1580–1954: A Descriptive Bibliography* (Athens: University of Georgia Press, 1974). The third important source is Harriet Merrifield Forbes's *New England Diaries, 1620-1800: A Descriptive Catalogue of Diaries, Orderly Books, and Sea Journals* (Topsfield, Mass.: privately printed, 1923). Despite some errors and inconsistencies—many of which have been corrected in Mathews's compilation of published diaries—Forbes's work remains a valuable source of information on New England diaries and the people who wrote them. Annotation of many of the entries contained in the following list may be found in the Mathews bibliography of published diaries and in Forbes. The latter also gives some limited genealogical information on the original authors.

338. Adams, Samuel. Surgeon. Conn. Diary, 1758-1819. Manuscript. NN.
339. Adlum, John. *Memoirs of the Life of John Adlum in the Revolutionary War.* Chicago: Caxton Club, 1968. 143 pp.
340. Alexander, Thomas. Capt. Mass. Journal, Ticonderoga and Canada, Mar.-Aug. 1776. In J. H. Temple and G. Sheldon, *A History of the Town of Northfield*, pp. 303-5. Albany, 1875.
341. Allan, John. Col. Me. "Allan's Journal [May 1777-Jan. 1778]." In Frederic Kidder, *Military Operations in Eastern Maine and Nova Scotia during the Revolution Chiefly Compiled from the Journals and Letters of Colonel John Allan*, pp. 91-163. Albany, 1867.
342. Allen, Daniel. Conn. Diary, Aug. 1776-Jan. 1777. In Edward C. Starr, *A History of Cornwall, Connecticut*, pp. 252-54. New Haven, 1920. CtCLA.
343. Allen, Ethan. Lt. Col. N.H. *A Narrative of Colonel Ethan Allen's Captivity . . . 1775, to . . . May, 1778.* Philadelphia, 1779. 46 pp. Also in Henry W. De Puy, *Ethan Allen and the Green-Mountain Heroes of '76* (Buffalo, 1861), pp. 213-73.
344. Allen, Ira. Maj. Gen. *Particulars of the Capture of the Ship "Olive Branch" . . . and a Narrative of Colonel Ethan Allen's Captivity, from 1775 to 1778.* Philadelphia, 1805. 551 pp.
345. Allen, Jacob [?]. Cpl. Mass. Diary, Oct. 1781-Sept. 1782. Manuscript. MTaHi.
346. Allen, Thomas. Chaplain. Mass. Diary, 1778-80. *Hartford [Conn.] Courant*, 1 Sept. 1877.
347. Anderson, Enoch. Capt. Del. *Personal Recollections of Captain Enoch Anderson, an Officer of the Delaware Regiments in the Revolutionary War.* Edited by Henry Hobart Bellas. Wilmington, 1896. 61 pp. Reprint ed., New York: Arno Press, 1971.

348. Anderson, Isaac. Lt. Ohio. Journal, Lochry's expedition into Ohio, Aug. 1781-July 1782. In James McBride, *Pioneer Biography*, pp. 278-85. Cincinnati, 1869. Extract in *Pennsylvania Archives*, 2d ser. 14:685-89. Also in *Publications of the Ohio State Archaeological and Historical Society* 6 (1898):389-92.

349. Anderson, Thomas. Lt. Del. "[Extracts from (?)] the Journal of Lieutenant Thomas Anderson of the Delaware Regiment, 1780-1782." *Historical Magazine*, 2d ser. 1 (1867):207-11. MdHi, DLC (Force transcripts).

350. Andros, Thomas. Privateer. *The "Old Jersey" Captive . . . on Board the "Old Jersey" Prison Ship at New York, 1781*. Boston, 1833. Reprinted in *Magazine of History*, extra no. 46.

351. Angell, Israel. Col. R.I. *Diary of Colonel Israel Angell, Commanding the Second Rhode Island Continental Regiment during the American Revolution, 1778-1781; Transcribed from the Original Manuscript, Together with a Biographical Sketch of the Author and Illustrative Notes*. Edited by Edward Field. Providence, 1899. 149 pp. Reprint ed., New York: Arno Press, 1971.

352. Armstrong, Samuel. Lt. Mass. Journal, Saratoga and Valley Forge, July 1777-June 1778. Manuscript. MBNEH.

353. Arnold, Benedict. Maj. Gen. Conn. "Benedict Arnold's Regimental Memorandum Book: Written while at Ticonderoga and Crown Point in 1775." *Pennsylvania Magazine of History and Biography* 8 (1884):363-76.

354. ———. "Arnold's Journal of His Expedition to Canada." In Justin H. Smith, *Arnold's March from Cambridge to Quebec*, pp. 45-61. New York: G. P. Putnam, 1938. Also in Kenneth Roberts, ed., *March to Quebec* (New York: Doubleday, Doran & Co., 1938), pp. 45-68. MH (Sparks manuscripts).

355. Atkins, Josiah. Conn. Extracts from journal, Jan.-Oct. 1781. Edited by Joseph Anderson. *The Town and City of Waterbury, Connecticut, from the Aboriginal Period to the Year Eighteen Hundred and Ninety-five*, 1:472-80. New Haven, 1896. CtNhHi.

356. Atlee, Samuel John. Col. Pa. "Col. Atlee's Journal of the Battle of Long Island, August 26, 1776." *Pennsylvania Archives*, 2d ser. 1: 509-16. Extracts in William B. Reed, *Life and Correspondence of Joseph Reed* (Philadelphia, 1847), 1:413-17.

357. Avery, David. Chaplain. Conn. Extracts from diary, siege of Boston, Apr.-May 1775. *American Monthly Magazine* 17 (1900): 342-47. CtHi.

358. ———. Extract from diary, 1776. *American Monthly Magazine* 19 (1901):20-23, 151-56, 260-62, 375-78. CtHi.

359. Avery, Rufus. Sgt. Conn. *See* 740.

360. Baldwin, Jeduthan. Col. Mass. *The Revolutionary Journal of Col. Jeduthan Baldwin.* Edited by Thomas W. Baldwin. Bangor, 1906. 164 pp. Reprint ed., New York: Arno Press, 1971. Extracts in *Bulletin of the Fort Ticonderoga Museum* 4 (1938):10-40. Also in *Journal of the Military Service Institute of the United States* 39:257-73.

361. Balme, Augustin Motten de la. Col. France. Diary, New England, May-Sept. 1779. Manuscript. BM, CaOOHa (copy).

362. Bangs, Isaac. Lt. Mass. *Journal of Lieutenant Isaac Bangs.* Edited by Edward Bangs. Cambridge, Mass., 1890. 70 pp. Reprint ed., New York: Arno Press, 1968. Extracts in *Proceedings of the New Jersey Historical Society* 8 (1856-59):120-25; *Historical Magazine*, 2d ser. 4 (1868):305-6. MHi.

363. Barber, Daniel. Pvt. Conn. *The History of My Own Times.* 3 vols. Washington, D.C., 1827-32. Extracts, 1775-76, *Historical Magazine* 7 (1863):82-88.

364. Barker, John. Lt. Journal, 1774-76. Manuscript. NN.

365. Barlow, Aaron. Sgt. Conn. "The March to Montreal and Quebec, [June-Dec.] 1775." *American Historical Register* 2 (1895):641-49.

366. Barr, John. Ens. N.Y. "Ensign John Barr's Book [1779-82]." In Almon W. Lauber, ed., *Orderly Books of the Fourth New York Regiment*, pp. 787-865. Albany: University of State of New York, 1932. N, DLC (copy).

367. Barringer, Rufus. Gen. Diary, 1770-78. Manuscript. Nc-Ar (copy).

368. Bartlett, Israel. Lt. Mass. Journal, New York, Oct.-Nov. 1777. In George W. Chase, *The History of Haverhill, Massachusetts, from Its First Settlement, in 1640, to the Year 1860*, pp. 401-2. Haverhill, 1861.

369. Barton, William. Lt. N.J. "Journal of Lieutenant William Barton, of Maxwell's Brigade; Kept during General Sullivan's Expedition against the Six Nations of Indians, [June-Oct.] 1779." *Proceedings of the New Jersey Historical Society* 2 (1846):22-42. Also in New York (State) Secretary of State, *Journals of the Military Expedition of Major General John Sullivan* (Auburn, 1887), pp. 3-14. NjHi.

370. Bates, Ambrose. Journal, Saratoga campaign, Aug.-Dec. 1777. In Edwin Victor Bigelow, *A Narrative History of the Town of Cohasset, Massachusetts*, pp. 299-303. Cohasset, 1898.

371. Bates, Issachar. *The Revolutionary War and Issachar Bates.* Chatham, N.Y.: Shaker Museum Foundation, 1960. 14 pp.

372. "Battle of Princeton, by a [New Jersey] Sergeant [Dec. 1776-Jan. 1777]." In Ebenezer Smith Thomas, *Reminiscences of the Last Sixty-five Years, Commencing with the Battle of Lexington...*, 1:283-87. Hartford, 1840.

373. Bayley, Frye. Ens. Vt. Journal, June 1776-Apr. 1783. In Frederick P. Wells, *History of Newbury, Vermont, from the Discovery of the Coös Country to Present Time; with Genealogical Records of Many Families,* pp. 382-84. St. Johnsbury, Vt.: Caledonian Co., 1902.

374. ————. *An Account by Frye Bayley of His Early Life, and His Services in the Revolutionary War, Written by Another Hand; Copied from a Manuscript in the Possession of the Massachusetts Historical Society.* Newbury, Vt., 1826-30. MHi, DLC (copy).

375. Beatty, Erkuries. Lt. Pa. "Journal of Lieut. Erkuries Beatty of the 4th Penn. Line [Apr.-Oct. 1779]." In New York (State) Secretary of State, *Journals of the Military Expedition of Major General John Sullivan,* pp. 15-37. Auburn, 1887. Also in *Pennsylvania Archives,* 2d ser. 15:219-53. NHi.

376. Beatty, William. Capt. Md. "Journal of Capt. William Beatty, [June] 1776-[Jan.] 1781." *Maryland Historical Magazine* 3 (1908): 104-19. Also in *Historical Magazine,* 2d ser. 1 (1867):17-85.

377. Becker, John P. Waggoner. N.Y. *The Sexagenary; or, Reminiscences of the American Revolution.* Albany, 1833. 203 pp. Reprint ed., Albany, 1866.

378. Bedinger, Henry. Sgt. Va. Journal, July 1775-June 1776. In Danske Dandridge, *Historic Shepardstown,* pp. 97-144. Charlottesville: Michie Co., 1910.

379. Beebe, Lewis. Surgeon. Mass. *Journal of Dr. Lewis Beebe: A Physician on the Expedition against Canada, 1776.* Edited by Frederick R. Kirkland. Philadelphia, 1935. 48 pp. Reprint ed., New York: Arno Press, 1971. Also in *Pennsylvania Magazine of History and Biography* 59 (1935):321-61.

380. Beekman, Tjerck. Lt. N.Y. "Journal of Lieutenant Tjerck Beekman, 1779: Of the Military Expedition of Major John Sullivan against the Six Nations of Indians." *Magazine of American History* 20 (1888): 127-36.

381. Beers, Nathan. Lt. Conn. Diary, Aug. 1777-Jan. 1782. Manuscript. DLC (Force transcripts).

382. Bemis, Phineas. Pvt. Mass. Journal, vicinity of Boston, Sept.-Nov. 1775. Manuscript. 21 pp. DNA (Pension files).

383. Benjamin, Samuel. Lt. Me. *Brief Notice of Lieutenant Samuel Benjamin, an Officer of the Revolutionary War, with Extracts from a Diary Kept by Him during the War.* Washington, D.C., 185-?. Also in Mary L. Benjamin, *Genealogy of the Family of Lieut. Samuel Benjamin* (n.p., 1900), pp. 24-38.

384. Berry, Joshua. N.H. Extract from journal, Nov. 1776. *Magazine of New England History* 2 (1892):192-93.

385. Besom, Philip. Privateer. Mass. "Captain Besom's Narrative [June 1775-Mar. 1783]." *Proceedings of the Massachusetts Historical Society* 5 (1860-62):357-60.

386. Bigelow, John. Maj. Conn. [?]. Abstract of the journal of Major John Bigelow, sent by Gates at Ticonderoga to Burgoyne in Canada, with dispatches from the Continental Congress, July-Aug. 1776. *American Historical Record* 1 (1872):438-40.

387. Biron, Armand Louis de Gontaut, Duc de Lauzun. Brig. Gen. France. *Memoirs of the Duc de Lauzun ... 1747-1783.* Translated by E. Jules Meras. New York: Sturgis & Waton Co., 1912. 364 pp. Also, C. K. Scott Moncrief, trans., *Memoirs of the Duc de Lauzun* (London: G. Routledge & Sons, 1928). Reprint ed., New York: Arno Press, 1969.

388. Bixby, Samuel. Pvt. Mass. "Diary of Samuel Bixby [May 1775-Jan. 1776]." *Proceedings of the Massachusetts Historical Society* 14 (1875-76):285-98.

389. Blake, Henry. Maj. Journal, 1776. Manuscript. [Mathews, *American Diaries in Manuscript* (entry 610), indicates that this privately held diary will be given to the New Hampshire Historical Society.] NhHi.

390. Blake, Thomas. Lt. N.H. "Lieutenant Thomas Blake's Journal [May 1777-Oct. 1780]." In Frederic Kidder, *History of the First New Hampshire Regiment,* pp. 25-56. Albany, 1868. Extract in New York (State) Secretary of State, *Journals of the Military Expedition of Major General John Sullivan* (Auburn, 1887), pp. 38-41. WHi.

391. Blanchard, Claude. Commissary. France. *The Journal of Claude Blanchard, Commissary of the French Auxiliary Army Sent to the United States during the American Revolution, 1780-1783.* Translated by William Duane. Edited by Thomas Balch. Albany, 1876. 207 pp. Reprint ed., New York: Arno Press, 1969. DLC.

392. Blatchford, John. Seaman. Mass. *Narrative of the Life and Captivity of John Blatchford . . . a Prisoner of War in the Late American Revolution.* New London, 1788. 23 pp. Also, Charles I. Bushnell, ed., *The Narrative of John Blatchford* (New York, 1865). Reprint ed., New York: Arno Press, 1971.

393. Bloomfield, Joseph. Capt. N.J. "Extracts from Captain Bloomfield's Journal [May 1776]." *Proceedings of the New Jersey Historical Society* 2 (1846-47):113-17. [This extract is a part of Ebenezer Elmer's journal. *See* 488.] NjHi, NjR (copy).

394. Boardman, Benjamin. Chaplain. Conn. "Diary of Rev. Benjamin Boardman [July-Nov. 1775]." *Proceedings of the Massachusetts Historical Society*, 2d ser. 7 (1891-92):400-413.

395. Boardman, Oliver. Conn. "Journal of Oliver Boardman of Middletown, [Sept.-Oct.] 1777, Burgoyne's Surrender." *Collections of the Connecticut Historical Society* 7 (1899):221-37.

396. Boudinot, Elias. Commissary-Gen. of Prisoners. N.J. *Journal; or, Historical Recollections of American Events during the Revolutionary War . . . Copied from His Own Original Manuscript.* Philadelphia, 1894. 97 pp. Reprint ed., New York: Arno Press, 1968. Extracts in *Pennsylvania Magazine of History and Biography* 15 (1891):27-34; 24 (1900):453-66.

397. Bowen, Ephraim, Jr. Capt. R.I. [?]. Journal, Oct.-Nov. 1775. In Peter Force, ed., *American Archives*, 4th ser. 3:1056-58 (note).

398. Bowman, Joseph. Maj. Va. "Journal of Joseph Bowman, [Jan.-Mar. 1779]." *Collections of the Illinois State History Library* 8 (1912): 155-64. WHi.

399. Boynton, Thomas. Sgt. Mass. "[Extract from] Thomas Boynton's Journal [Apr.-Aug. 1775]." *Proceedings of the Massachusetts Historical Society* 15 (1876-77):254-55. Extract in Sarah Loring Bailey, *Historical Sketches of Andover* (Boston, 1880), pp. 321-22. MHi.

400. Bradbury, John. Lt. Me. Diary, 1760-1813. Manuscript. MeHi.

401. Bradford, Thomas. Pvt. Conn. Journal and account book, Feb. 1776-Apr. 1786. Manuscript. 15 pp. DNA (Pension files).

402. Bradford, William. Col. Pa. [?]. Diary. Manuscript. PHi.

403. Brahm, Ferdinand de. Maj. Germany. "Journal of the Siege of Charleston by the English in 1780; The Army Commanded by Gen. Sir Henry Clinton, and the Fleet by Admiral Arbuthnot; The Garrison by Major-General Lincoln." Translated by James Ferguson. In R. W. Gibbes, *Documentary History of the American Revolution . . . 1776-1782*, pp. 124-28. New York, 1857.

404. Broglie, Claude Victor, Prince de. Col. France. "Narrative of the Prince de Broglie." Translated by E. W. Balch. In *Magazine of American History* 1, pt. 1 (1877):180-86, 231-35, 306-9, 374-80.

405. Brooke, Francis Taliaferro. Lt. Va. *A Narrative of My Life, for My Family*. Richmond, 1849. 90 pp. Reprinted as "A Family Narrative," *Magazine of History*, extra no. 74. Reprint ed., New York: Arno Press, 1971.

406. Broome, L. Sgt. Diary, 1780-81 [?]. Manuscript. 29 pp. NWM (Copy).

407. Brown, John. Ens. N.C. Militia diary, 1776-78. DLC.

408. Brown, Moses. Capt. Journal, New York-New Jersey campaign, 1776. Manuscript. MBNEH (copy).

409. Brown, Obadiah. "Military Journal, January, 1776-January, 1777, around Boston and New York." *Quarterly Bulletin of the Westchester County Historical Society* 4 (1928):67-72; 5 (1929):10-20.

410. Brown, Tarleton. Capt. Va. *Memoirs of Tarleton Brown, a Captain in the Revolutionary Army*. Edited by Charles I. Bushnell. New York, 1862. 65 pp.

411. Buell, John Hutchinson. Capt. Conn. "A Fragment from the Diary of Major John Hutchinson Buell, U.S.A., Who Joined the American Army at the Beginning of the Revolutionary War and Remained in Service until 1803." *Journal of the Military Service Institute of the United States* 40 (1907):102-13, 206-68.

412. Burnham, John. Maj. Mass. *Recollections of the Revolutionary War, from Bunker Hill to Yorktown: Narrative of Major John Burnham, a Gloucester Soldier, Who Served from May, 1775, to January, 1784*. Gloucester, Mass., 1881. 16 pp. Reprinted in *Magazine of History*, extra no. 54.

413. Burnham, Jonathan. Col. Mass. *The Life of Col. Jonathan Burnham, Now Living in Salisbury, Mass.; Being a Narrative of His Long and Useful Life*. Portsmouth, N.H., 1814. 8 pp. Reprint ed., Salem, Mass, 1909.

414. Burrowes (Burrows), John. Maj. N.J. "Journal of Major John Burrowes [Aug.-Oct. 1779]." In New York (State) Secretary of State, *Journals of the Military Expedition of Major General John Sullivan*, pp. 43-51. Auburn, 1887. NBuHi (copy).

415. Burrows, John. Gen. Pa. *Sketch of the Life of Gen. John Burrows, of Lycoming County*. N.p., 1837 [?]. 13 pp. Reprint ed., Williamsport, Pa., 1917.

416. Burton, John. Lt. N.H. "Diaries [i.e., orderly book and diary] of

Lieut. Jonathan Burton, of Welton, N.H. [Aug.-Nov. 1776]." *Provincial and State Papers of New Hampshire* 14 (1885):677-702. NhHi.

417. Butler, Richard. Col. Pa. Journals, 1754-88. Manuscript. WHi.

418. ———. Journal of negotiations with Indians, 1775. Manuscript. PHi.

419. ———. Journal, siege of Yorktown, Sept.-Oct. 1781. *Virginia Historical Magazine* 8 (1864):102-12.

420. Calfe, John. Capt. N.H. Journal, Feb.-Aug. 1777. In Harriette Eliza Noyes, *A Memorial of the Town of Hampstead, New Hampshire: Historic and Genealogic Sketches* ..., 1:288-94. Boston, 1899-1903.

421. "Camp Life in 1776—Siege of Boston." [Edited extracts from a manuscript journal, by a lieutenant in a Connecticut regiment, Apr. 1776.] *Historical Magazine* 8 (1864):326-32.

422. Campbell, McDonald. N.J. *The Life and Adventures of M'D. Campbell; The Money-Maker.* N.p., n.d. [Mark Edward Lender, "The Enlisted Line ... ," (Ph. D. diss., Rutgers University, 1975) states this is "a rare privately printed memoir ... held by the Special Collections of Rutgers University."]

423. Campfield, Jabez. Surgeon. N.J. "Diary of Dr. Jabez Campfield, Surgeon in Spencer's Regiment While Attached to Sullivan's Expedition against the Indians, from May 23rd to October 2nd, 1779." *Proceedings of the New Jersey Historical Society*, 2d ser. 3 (1872-74): 115-36. Also in New York (State) Secretary of State, *Journals of the Military Expedition of Major General John Sullivan* (Auburn, 1887), pp. 52-61. NjHi.

424. Carpenter, Jonathan. Mass. "[Extract from the] Diary of Jonathan Carpenter [Feb. 1778-Nov. 1780]." *Proceedings of the Vermont Historical Society*, 1872, pp. vii-xi.

425. Castries, Armand Charles Augustin de la Croix, Duc de. Col. France. "Journal de mon voyage en Amérique [Mar.-Sept. 1780]." Manuscript. 76 pp. MiU-C (copy).

426. Chamberlain, William. Pvt. Mass. "Letter [i.e., an incomplete autobiography, partly covering military service 1775-77] of General William Chamberlain." *Proceedings of the Massachusetts Historical Society*, 2d ser. 10 (1895-96):490-504.

427. Chambers, John. Capt. Pa. See 579.

428. Chandler, Abiel. Fifer. Mass. "Revolutionary Journal Kept by Abiel Chandler of Andover, from December 2, 1776 until April 1, 1777, during Service on the North River, New York." *Historical Collections of the Essex Institute* 47 (1911): 181-86. MSaE.

429. Chapin, Noah, Jr. Ens. Conn. Journal, Apr.-July 1775. Manuscript. Ct, MBAt (copy).
430. Chase, Samuel. Pvt. N.H. Journals, Aug.-Oct. 1779, July 1781-Jan. 1782, May 1782-Apr. 1787. Manuscript. 71 pp. DNA (Pension files).
431. Childs, Reuben. Pvt. Mass. Journal, Dec. 1776-Jan. 1777. Manuscript. 1 p. DNA (Pension files).
432. Chilton, John. Capt. Va. "The Diary of Captain John Chilton, 3d Virginia Regt. [Jan.-Sept. 1777]." *Tyler's Quarterly Historical and Genealogical Magazine* 12 (1931):283-89.
433. Clap, Caleb. Ens. Mass. "Diary of Ensign Caleb Clap of Colonel Baldwin's Regiment, Massachusetts Line, Continental Army, March 29 until October 23, 1776." *Historical Magazine*, 3d ser. 3 (1874-75): 133-37, 247-51.
434. Clap, Daniel. Journal, Sullivan's expedition. Manuscript. ICN.
435. Clark, Elihu, Jr. Pvt. Conn. Journal, siege of Boston, Apr.-Dec. 1775. Manuscript. DLC (Force transcripts).
436. Clark, George Rogers. Col. Va. "Clark's 'Diary,' December 25, 1776 to March 30, 1778." *Collections of the Illinois State History Library* 8 (1912):20-28.
437. ———. "Journal of Colonel Clark [Feb. 1779]." *Collections of the Illinois State History Library* 8 (1912):164-68. Also in *American Historical Review* 1 (1895):90-94. WHi.
438. ———. "Clark's Memoir, 1773-1779." *Collections of the Illinois State History Library* 8 (1912):208-302. Also in Henry Pirtle, ed., *Col. George Rogers Clark's Sketch of His Campaign in the Illinois in 1778-9* (Cincinnati, 1869).
439. Clark, Jonathan. Lt. Col. Va. Diary, 1770-1811. Manuscript. KyLoF.
440. Clark, Joseph. Officer. N.J. "Diary of Joseph Clark, Attached to the Continental Army, from May, 1778, to November, 1779." *Proceedings of the New Jersey Historical Society* 7 (1854):93-110.
441. Cleaves, Nathan. Journal, May 1775-Jan. 1776. Manuscript. MSaE (copy).
442. Cleveland, John. Chaplain. Conn. Journal, 1776. Manuscript. DLC.
443. Closen, Ludwig von, Baron. Capt. France. *The Revolutionary Journal of Baron Ludwig von Closen, 1780-1783.* Edited and translated by Evelyn M. Acomb. Chapel Hill: University of North Carolina Press, 1958. 382 pp. DLC (copy).

444. Cobb, David. Lt. Col. Mass. Extracts from journal, Oct.-Nov. 1781. *Proceedings of the Massachusetts Historical Society* 19 (1881-82):67-72.

445. Colbrath, William. Journal, Fort Schuyler, 1777. Manuscript. NN.

446. Collins, James Potter. *Autobiography of a Revolutionary Soldier.* Clinton, La., 1859. 176 pp.

447. Connor, Timothy. Privateer. "A Yankee Privateersman in Prison in England, 1777-1779." *New England Historical and Genealogical Register* 30 (1876):174-77; 31 (1877):212-13, 284-88; 32 (1878):70-73, 165-68, 280-85; 33 (1879):18-20, 36-41. [The manuscript of this journal, along with a companion volume of songs and ballads is in the Manuscript Division, Library of Congress, where authorship is given for both as "Anonymous, American Prisoners."] DLC.

448. Corbett, Ichabod. Pvt. Mass. "Diary of Ichabod Corbett of Mendon, Mass." *Proceedings of the Worcester Society of Antiquity* 19 (1903):171-86.

449. Cornelius, Elias. Surgeon. R.I. *Journal of Dr. Elias Cornelius, a Revolutionary Surgeon: Graphic Description of His Sufferings While a Prisoner in Provost Jail, New York, 1777 and 1778, with Biographical Sketch.* Washington, D.C.: privately printed, 1903. 27 pp.

450. Cowan, John. Capt. Journal, Kentucky, Mar.-Sept. 1777. In Willard R. Jillson, *Tales of the Dark and Bloody Ground ...*, pp. 63-68. Louisville: C. T. Dearling, 1930. WHi (copy).

451. Cowdrey, Nathaniel. Capt. Mass. "Nathaniel Cowdrey of Reading, Mass. [with a fascimile of his journal, July-Dec. 1780]." *American Monthly Magazine* 4 (1894):409-16.

452. Craft, Benjamin. Lt. Mass. "Craft's Journal of the Siege of Boston [June-Nov. 1775]." Edited by S. P. Fowler. *Historical Collections of the Essex Institute* 3 (1861):51-57, 133-40, 167-74, 219-20.

453. Craft, Eleazer. Maj. Mass. "Journal of Eleazer Craft, [Sept.-Dec. 1777]." *Historical Collections of the Essex Institute* 6 (1864):194-98. Also in James M. Crafts and William F. Crafts, *The Crafts Family: A Genealogical and Biographical History* (Northampton, Mass., 1893), pp. 689-93. MSaE.

454. Crocker, E. Capt. Journal, New York and vicinity, fall 1776. Manuscript. MeHi.

455. Croghan, William. Journal, campaign in New Jersey, 1776-77. Manuscript. WHi.

456. ———. Journal, march from New Jersey to South Carolina. Manuscript. WHi.

457. ———. Journal, 1780. Manuscript. MH (Sparks manuscripts).

458. ———. Journal, 1781. Manuscript. WHi.

459. Crosby, Enoch. Spy. *The Spy Unmasked; or, Memoirs of Enoch Crosby, alias Harvey Birch.* Compiled by H. L. Barnum. New York, 1828. 206 pp.

460. Cross, Ralph. Lt. Col. Mass. "The Journal of Ralph Cross, of Newburyport, Who Commanded the Essex Regiment, at the Surrender of Burgoyne in 1777." *Historical Magazine,* 2d ser. 7 (1870): 8-11.

461. Curtin, Daniel M. Journal, siege of Boston and march to New York, 1775-76. Manuscript. NjHi.

462. Cushing, Charles. Capt. Mass. Journal, retreat from Canada, June-Sept. 1776. Manuscript. DLC (Force transcripts).

463. Cutler, Manasseh. Chaplain. Mass. In William Parker Cutler and Julia Perkins Cutler, *Life, Journals and Correspondence of Rev. Manasseh Cutler, LL.D.,* 1:46-76. Cincinnati, 1888.

464. Cutler, Samuel. Privateer. Mass. "Prison Ships, and the 'Old Mill Prison,' Plymouth, England, [extracts from diary, Nov. 1776-Nov.] 1777." *New England Historical and Genealogical Register* 32 (1878): 42-44, 184-88, 305-8, 395-98.

465. Danforth, Joshua. Col. Mass. Journal, Mar.-Oct. 1776. *American Monthly Magazine* 1 (1892):619-20.

466. Davis, John. Capt. Pa. "The Yorktown Campaign: Journal of Captain John Davis of the Pennsylvania Line [May-Dec. 1781]." *Pennsylvania Magazine of History and Biography* 5 (1881):290-310. Also in *Virginia Magazine of History and Biography* 1 (1893):2-16. NSchHi.

467. Davis, Joshua. Privateer. Mass. *A Narrative of Joshua Davis, an American Citizen, Who Was Pressed and Served on Board Six Ships of the British Navy [June 1779-Dec. 1787].* Boston, 1811. 72 pp.

468. Davis, Nathan. Pvt. N.H. "History of Expedition against the Five Nations, Commanded by General John Sullivan, in 1779." *Historical Magazine,* 2d ser. 3 (1868):198-205.

469. Deall, Daniel. Pvt. Pa. Journal, 1776-1810, including service at Fort Trumbull, Sept.-Nov. 1776. Manuscript. 52 pp. DNA (Pension files).

470. Dearborn, Henry. Lt. Col. N.H. *Revolutionary War Journals of Henry Dearborn, 1775-1783.* Chicago: Caxton Club, 1939. 264 pp. Also in *Proceedings of the Massachusetts Historical Society,* 2d ser. 2 (1885-86):275-305; 3 (1886-87):102-33. Extract in New York (State)

Secretary of State, *Journals of the Military Expedition of Major General John Sullivan* (Auburn, 1887), pp. 62-79. Extract in Kenneth Roberts, ed., *March to Quebec* (New York: Doubleday, Doran & Co., 1938), pp. 129-68. MB, NN.

471. de Gallatin, Gaspard, Baron. Lt. Switzerland. *Journal of the Siege of Yorktown.* Translated by William and Mary College, French Department. Washington, D.C.: Government Printing Office, 1931. 15 pp. DLC.

472. Denny, David. Capt. Pa. Diary, Apr. 1811-Feb. 1820. Manuscript. 9 pp. DNA (Pension files).

473. Denny, Ebenezer. Maj. Pa. "Military Journal of Major Ebenezer Denny [May 1781-May 1795]." *Memoirs of the Historical Society of Pennsylvania* 7 (1860): 205-409. Reprint ed., New York: Arno Press, 1971. WHi.

474. d'Estaing, Charles Henri Theodat, Comte. Adm. France. Journal, 1778-79. Manuscript. PHi. [Philip Hamer, *Guide to Archives and Manuscripts in the United States* (New Haven: Yale University Press, 1961), notes this as a letter book, not a journal.]

475. Deux-Ponts, Guillaume de Forbach, Comte de. Col. France. *My Campaigns in America: A Journal Kept by Count William Deux-Ponts, 1780-1781.* Translated and edited by Samuel Abbot Greene. Boston, 1868. 176 pp.

476. Dewees, Samuel. Pvt. Pa. *A History of the Life and Services of Captain Samuel Dewees . . . the Whole Written (in Part from Manuscript in the Hand Writing of Captain Dewees,) . . . by John Smith Hanna.* Baltimore, 1844. 360 pp.

477. Dewey, John. Pvt. Mass. Journal, New York and New Jersey, Apr. 1776-Feb. 1777. In Adelbert M. Dewey and Louis M. Dewey, *Life of George Dewey, Rear Admiral, U.S.N.; and Dewey Family History*, pp. 278-81. Westfield, Mass., 1898.

478. Dewey, Russell. Adj. Mass. Journal, march to Quebec, Jan.-Apr. 1776. In Adelbert M. Dewey and Louis M. Dewey, *Life of George Dewey, Rear Admiral, U.S.N.; and Dewey Family History*, pp. 266-71. Westfield, Mass., 1898. Also in John Hoyt Lockwood, *Westfield [Mass.] and Its Historic Influences 1699-1919 . . .* (Westfield, Mass.: privately printed, 1922), pp. 590-96. MWeAt.

479. "A Diary of the Siege of Fort Schuyler [Apr.-Aug. 1777]." *Magazine of History* 3 (1906): 90-104.

480. Dimock, David. Lt. Extracts from journal, battles of Long Island and Harlem Heights, Aug. and Oct. 1776. *American Monthly Magazine* 1 (1892): 353-54.

481. Dorr, William. Diary, march to Quebec, 1775. Manuscript. MHi.

482. "The Doughboy of 1780, Pages from a Revolutionary Diary." Edited by James R. Nichols. *Atlantic Monthly* 134 (1924): 459-63.

483. du Bourg, Cromot, Baron. Capt. France. "Diary of a French Officer [Mar.-Nov.] 1781 (Presumed to be that of Baron Cromot du Bourg, Aid to Rochambeau)." *Magazine of American History* 4 (1880):205-14, 293-308, 376-85, 441-49.

484. Duncan, James. Capt. Pa. "Diary of Captain James Duncan, of Colonel Moses Hazen's Regiment in the Yorktown Campaign, [Oct.] 1781." *Pennsylvania Archives*, 2d ser. 15:743-52. Also in *Magazine of History* 2 (1905): 407-16.

485. Dwinnell, Solomon. Diary, 1777. Manuscript. MnHi (copy).

486. Eaton, Isaiah. Pvt. and artificer. Mass. Journal, Mar.-June 1776. Manuscript. 12 pp. DNA (Pension files).

487. Elkins, Jonathan. "Reminiscences of Jonathan Elkins: A Manuscript [1775-81]." *Proceedings of the Vermont Historical Society*, 1919-20, pp. 187-211.

488. Elmer, Ebenezer. Surgeon. N.J. "Journal Kept during an Expedition to Canada in 1776." Continued as "Journal of Lieutenant Ebenezer Elmer of the Third Regiment of New Jersey Troop in the Continental Service [Mar. 1776-May 1777, Aug. 1782-Nov. 1783]." *Proceedings of the New Jersey Historical Society* 2 (1846-47): 95-146, 150-94; 3 (1848-49): 90-102. NjHi.

489. ———. "The Lost Pages of Elmer's Journal [Oct.-Nov. 1776]." *Proceedings of the New Jersey Historical Society*, 2d ser. 10 (1925): 410-24. NjHi.

490. ———. "Extracts from the Journal of Surgeon Ebenezer Elmer of the New Jersey Continental Line, September 11-19, 1777." *Pennsylvania Magazine of History and Biography* 35 (1911): 103-7.

491. ———. "Extracts from a Journal Kept by Doctor Ebenezer Elmer During Sullivan's Expedition [June-Aug. 1779]." *Proceedings of the New Jersey Historical Society* 2 (1846-47): 43-50. Reprinted in New York (State) Secretary of State, *Journals of the Military Expedition of Major General John Sullivan* (Auburn, 1887), pp. 80-85. WHi.

492. Emerson, Daniel. Chaplain. N.H. Journal, Crown Point, July-Sept. 1775. In Benjamin K. Emerson, *The Ipswitch Emersons . . . : A Genealogy*, pp. 86-91. Boston: privately printed, 1900.

493. Emerson, William. Mass. Extract from diary, Concord, 19 Apr. 1775. In *The Literature of the Nineteenth of April*. Concord, Mass., 1876.

494. Erickson, Michael. Sgt. N.J. Journal, march to join Sullivan's expedition, May-Aug. 1779. Manuscript. DLC.

495. Everett, Abner. Lt. Pa. Journal, New York campaign, subsequent capture at Fort Washington and imprisonment, July 1776-May 1780. Manuscript. 18 pp. DNA (Pension files).

496. Ewing, George. Ens. N.J. *The Military Journal of George Ewing (1754-1824), a Soldier of Valley Forge* [*Nov. 1775-May 1778*]. Yonkers, N.Y.: privately printed, 1928. 54 pp. Extracts in *American Monthly Magazine* 37 (1910): 471-73; 38 (1911): 5-8, 50-53.

497. Fairbanks, John. Privateer. Mass. "John Fairbanks — His Journal — The Privateer *Wasp* Journal [July-Sept. 1782]." *Collections and Proceedings of the Maine Historical Society*, 2d ser. 6 (1895): 139-44.

498. Fairies, Arthur. S.C. Journal of a campaign against Indians, July-Oct. 1776. Manuscript. 72 pp. DNA (Pension files).

499. Fairlie, James. Lt. N.Y. "Journal of Lieutenant James Fairlie of the Second New York Regiment, August 26 to September 8, 1779." In New York (State) Division of Archives and History, *The Sullivan-Clinton Campaign in 1779*, pp. 175-78. Albany, 1929. N.

500. Fanning, Nathaniel. Capt. Conn. *Memoirs of the Life of Captain Nathaniel Fanning, an American Navy Officer, Who Served during Part of the American Revolution under the Command of Commodore John Paul Jones, Esq.* New York, 1808. 270 pp. Also, *Fanning's Narrative; Being the Memoirs of Nathaniel Fanning, an Officer of the Revolutionary Navy, 1778-1783*, edited by John S. Barnes (New York: Naval Historical Society, 1912), 258 pp. Reprint ed., New York: Arno Press, 1968.

501. Farnsworth, Amos. Lt. Mass. "Diary Kept by Lieut. Amos Farnsworth of Groton, Mass., during a Part of the Revolutionary War; April, 1775-May, 1779." Edited by Samuel A. Greene. Cambridge, Mass., 1898. 36 pp. Also in *Proceedings of the Massachusetts Historical Society*, 2d ser. 12 (1897-99): 74-107.

502. Farnsworth, William. 1st Lt. Mass. Travel log, Dec. 1776-Jan. 1777. Manuscript. 7 pp. DNA (Pension files).

503. Farnum, Benjamin. Lt. Diary, northern campaign, 1777-78. Manuscript. MHi.

504. Fassett, John. Capt. Vt. Journal, march to Quebec, Sept.-Dec. 1775. In Harry Parker Ward, *The Follett-Dewey-Fassett-Safford Ancestry of Captain Martin Dewey (1765-1831)*, pp. 215-43. Columbus, Ohio, 1896.

505. Fay, Hezekiah. Pvt. Mass. Journal, New York City and West Point, Aug.-Oct. 1780. Manuscript. 23 pp. DNA (Pension files).

506. Fellows, Moses. Sgt. N.H. "Journal of Sergeant Moses Fellows [June–Sept. 1779]." In New York (State) Secretary of State, *Journals of the Military Expedition of Major General John Sullivan*, pp. 86–91. Auburn, 1887.

507. Feltman, William. Lt. Pa. "The Journal of Lieut. William Feltman, of the First Pennsylvania Regiment, from May 26, 1781 to April 25, 1782, Embracing the Siege of Yorktown and the Southern Campaign." *Collections of the Historical Society of Pennsylvania* 1 (1853): 303–48. Reprint ed., New York: Arno Press, 1971. PHi. *See also* 661.

508. Few, William. Col. Ga. "Autobiography of William Few of Georgia." *Magazine of American History* 7 (1881): 343–58.

509. Fisher, Elijah. Pvt. Me. *Elijah Fisher's Journal while in the War for Independence, and Continued Two Years after He Came to Maine, 1775–1784.* Augusta, Me., 1880. 29 pp. Reprinted in *Magazine of History*, extra no. 6. MeHi.

510. Fisher, John. Pvt. Conn. "John Fisher's Reminiscences of the Revolution [July–Oct. 1775, June–July 1777]." *Magazine of History* 13 (1911): 184–86.

511. Fitch, Jabez. Lt. Conn. "A Journal from August 5th to December 13th, 1775." *Proceedings of the Massachusetts Historical Society*, 2d ser. 9 (1894–95): 41–91. DLC (Force transcripts).

512. ———. Diary, Jan.–Apr. 1776. Manuscript. DLC (Force transcripts).

513. ———. *The New York Diary of Lieutenant Jabez Fitch of the 17th (Connecticut) Regiment from August 22, 1776 to December 15, 1777.* Edited by W. H. W. Sabine. New York: Colburn & Tegg, 1954. 256 pp. Reprint ed., New York: Arno Press, 1971. Extracts reprinted as *Prison Ship Martyr* (Brooklyn, 1897). NN.

514. Fitch, Zachariah. Capt. Mass. Travel log, march from Groton to Ticonderoga, Aug. 1776 [?]. Manuscript. MHi.

515. Fithian, Philip Vickers. Chaplain [?]. N.J. *Philip Vickers Fithian: Journal 1775–1776, Written on the Virginia-Pennsylvania Frontier and in the Army around New York.* Edited by Robert G. Albion and Leonidas Dodson. Princeton: Princeton University Press, 1934.

516. Fitts, Abraham. Lt. N.H. Journal, Saratoga campaign, Sept.–Nov. 1777. In Jacob Bailey Moore, *History of the Town of Candia, ... N.H., from Its First Settlement to the Present Time*, pp. 81–84. Manchester, N.H., 1893.

517. Flanders, John. Prison diary, Quebec, Jan.–Apr. 1776. In Charles Carleton Coffin, *The History of Boscawen and Webster [N.H.] from 1773 to 1878*, pp. 250–51. Concord, N.H., 1878.

518. Fletcher, Ebenezer. Fifer. N.H. *A Narrative of the Captivity and Sufferings of Mr. Ebenezer Fletcher of New-Ipswich, Who Was Wounded at Hubbardston, in the Year 1777 and Taken Prisoner by the British.* Amherst, N.H., 1798. 26 pp. 4th ed. rev. New Ipswich, N.H., 1827. Also in *Magazine of History*, extra no. 151.

519. Fobes, Simon. Pvt. Conn. "Journal of a Member of Arnold's Expedition to Quebec (1775)." *Historical Collections of the Mahoning Valley Historical Society* (1876), pp. 345-94. Reprinted in *Magazine of History*, extra no. 130. Also in Kenneth Roberts, ed., *March to Quebec* (New York: Doubleday, Doran & Co., 1938), pp. 573-613.

520. Fogg, Jeremiah. Maj. N.H. *Journal of Major Jeremiah Fogg, during the Expedition of Gen. Sullivan in 1779, against the Western Indians.* Exeter, N.H., 1879. 24 pp. Also in New York (State) Secretary of State, *Journals of the Military Expedition of Major General John Sullivan* (Auburn, 1887), pp. 92-101.

521. Foot, Caleb. Pvt. and privateer. Mass. "Reminiscences of the Revolution: Prison Letters and Sea Journal of Caleb Foot [Oct. 1775-Jan. 1782]." Compiled by Caleb Foote. *Historical Collections of the Essex Institute* 26 (1889): 90-120.

522. Foster, Thomas. Pvt. [?]. Mass. Journal, 1779-80. Manuscript. CSmH.

523. Fowler, Theodosius. Capt. N.Y. *Memoir of Theodosius Fowler, Late Captain in the Second New York Regiment of Continental Troops.* New York, 1859. 15 pp.

524. Fox, Ebenezer. Seaman. Mass. *The Revolutionary Adventures of Ebenezer Fox [1775-83].* Boston, 1838. 238 pp. Reprinted as *The Adventures of Ebenezer Fox in the Revolutionary War* (Boston, 1848), 240 pp.

525. Francis, Ebenezer. Col. Mass. [?]. Diary, 1776. Manuscript. NIC.

526. Frisbie, Judah. Conn. Journal, Apr.-Dec. 1773, May–Sept. 1776. In Samuel Orcutt, *History of the Town of Wolcott (Connecticut) from 1731 to 1874 . . . with Genealogies of the Families of the Town,* pp. 306-10. Waterbury, Conn., 1874.

527. *From Cambridge to Champlain, March 18 to May 5, 1776.* Edited by Lawrence B. Romaine. Middleboro, Mass.: Weathercock House, 1957. 21 pp.

528. Gale, Edmund. Journal, 1780-81. Manuscript. NHi.

529. Gallup, Nehemiah. Pvt. Conn. Journal, march from Connecticut to New York City, Sept.-Nov. 1776. Manuscript. DLC.

530. Gannett, Deborah (Sampson). Pvt. Mass. *An Address Deliv-*

ered ... at Boston ... by Mrs. Deborah Gannett, the American Heroine, Who Served Three Years with Reputation (Undiscovered as a Female) in the Late American Army. Dedham, Mass., 1802. 14 pp. Reprint ed., Boston: Sharon Historical Society, 1905. Reprinted in *Magazine of History*, extra no. 124.

531. Gano, John. Chaplain. N.Y. *Biographical Memoirs of the Late Rev. John Gano.* New York, 1806. Revolutionary war portions, 1776-83, in *Historical Magazine* 5 (1861): 330-35.

532. Gaston, Joseph. S.C. "A Reminiscence of the War of the Revolution, in South Carolina [1780]." *Historical Magazine*, 3d ser. 2 (1873): 90-92.

533. Gay, Fisher. Lt. Col. Conn. "[Extract from] Diary of Lieutenant-Colonel Fisher Gay [Feb.-Mar. 1776]." *Magazine of American History*, 8, pt. 1 (1882): 127-29.

534. Gerrish, Henry. Capt. N.H. Journal, Apr. 1775-Oct. 1777. In Charles Carleton Coffin, *The History of Boscawen and Webster [N.H.] from 1733 to 1878,* pp. 247, 265. Concord, N.H., 1878.

535. Gerrish, Jacob. Journal, New York, Aug. Nov. 1776. *Putnam's Monthly Historical Magazine* 3 (1895): 220-23.

536. Gibbs, Caleb. Maj. Mass. Journal, march from New Jersey to New York, Apr.-Nov. 1780. Manuscript. Interleaved in *Continental Pocket Almanac* (1780). DLC.

537. ———. "Part of a Diary of Major Gibbs, [Aug.] 1778." *Pennsylvania Archives*, 1st ser. 6:734-36.

538. Giffen, Simon. Sgt. Maj. Conn. Journal, 1777-79. Manuscript. Ct, CtY.

539. Gilbert, Benjamin. Col. [?]. Journal, 1778-88. Manuscript. NCooHi.

540. Gilbert, James. Mass. Journal, New York, July-Sept. 1775. *Magazine of New England History* 3 (1893): 188.

541. Gile, Ezekiel. Maj. N.H. Journal, May 1778-June 1780. *Boston Transcript*, 4 Dec. 1905.

542. Goodhue, Joseph. Pvt. Mass. Fragmentary autobiographical notes. *History and Proceedings of the Pocumtuck Valley Memorial Association* 3 (1890): 7.

543. Goodwin, John. Lt. Mass. "Military Journal Kept in 1777, during the Rhode Island Expedition, by John Goodwin of Marblehead, Mass., First Lieutenant in Capt. Nathaniel Lindsey's Company in Col. Timothy Pickering's Regiment." *Historical Collections of the Essex Institute* 45 (1909): 205-11.

544. Gookin, Daniel. Ens. N.H. "Revolutionary Journal of Daniel Gookin, [May-Sept.] 1779." *New England Historical and Genealogical Register* 16 (1862): 27-33. Also in New York (State) Secretary of State, *Journals of the Military Expedition of Major General John Sullivan* (Auburn, 1887), pp. 102-6.

545. Gore, Obadiah. Lt. Pa. "Diary of Obadiah Gore in the Sullivan Expedition, [July-Sept.] 1779." *Proceedings and Collections of the Wyoming Historical and Geological Society* 19 (1926): 219-35. Also in *Bulletin of the New York Public Library* 33 (1929): 711-42. Also in New York (State) Division of Archives and History, *The Sullivan-Clinton Campaign in 1779* (Albany, 1929), pp. 179-88. MH (Sparks manuscripts).

546. Grant, George. Sgt. Maj. N.J. "March of Sullivan's Army in [May-Dec.] 1779." *Hazard's Register of Pennsylvania* 14 (1834): 72-76. Reprinted in New York (State) Secretary of State, *Journals of the Military Expedition of Major General John Sullivan* (Auburn, 1887), pp. 108-14.

547. Grant, Thomas. Surveyor. "A Jurnal of Janaral Sullivan's Army after They Left Wyoming, [July-Sept. 1779]." *Historical Magazine* 6 (1862): 233-37, 273-76. Reprinted in New York (State) Secretary of State, *Journals of the Military Expedition of Major General John Sullivan* (Auburn, 1887), pp. 137-44.

548. Graton, Thomas. Pvt. and artificer. Mass. Journal, Aug. 1767-Sept. 1790. Manuscript. 34 pp. DNA (Pension files).

549. Graves, Daniel. Mass. Journal, New York, Dec. 1776-Mar. 1777. *Quarterly Bulletin of the Westchester County Historical Society* 10 (1934): 45-48.

550. Gray, David. Pvt. [?] and spy. *Gray's Narrative.* N.p., 1825 [?]. 8 pp.

551. Graydon, Alexander. Capt. Pa. *Memoirs of a Life, Chiefly Passed in Pennsylvania.* Harrisburg, 1811. 378 pp. Also, *Memoirs of His Own Time, with Reminiscences of the Men and Events of the Revolution,* edited by John Stockton Littell (Philadelphia, 1846). Reprint ed., New York: Arno Press, 1969.

552. Greele, Thomas. Shipmaster. Mass. Sea journal, Mar.-June 1779. In John J. Currier, *History of Newburyport, Mass., 1764-1909,* pp. 631-32. Newburyport, Mass.: privately printed, 1906-9.

553. Green, Ezra. Surgeon. N.H. *Diary of Ezra Green, M.D., Surgeon on Board the Continental Ship-of-War "Ranger," under John Paul Jones, from November 1, 1777, to September 27, 1778.* Boston, 1875. 28 pp. Reprint ed., New York: Arno Press, 1971.

554. Greenleaf, Moses. Capt. Mass. Diary. Manuscript. 35 pp. MHi.

555. Greenwood, John. Pvt. N.Y. *The Revolutionary Services of John Greenwood of Boston and New York, 1775-1783.* Edited by Isaac J. Greenwood. New York: DeVinne Press, 1922. 155 pp.

556. Grimke, John Foucheraud. Maj. S.C. "Journal of the Campaign to the Southward, May 9th to July 14th, 1778." *South Carolina Historical and Genealogical Magazine* 12 (1911): 60-69, 118-34, 190-206.

557. Guild, Joseph. Capt. Mass. Extracts from diary, Apr. 1776-July 1777 [?]. *Dedham Historical Register* 7 (1896): 45-47.

558. Hagen, Edmund. Surgeon [?]. Me. Prison diary of a captured privateer, Oct.-Dec. 1776. *American Monthly Magazine* 24 (1904): 14-16, 110-11.

559. Hale, Nathan. Capt. Conn. Journal, Sept. 1775-Aug. 1776. In I. W. Stuart, *Life of Captain Nathan Hale*, pp. 205-26. Hartford, 1856. Also in Henry Phelps Johnston, *Nathan Hale 1776: Biography and Memorials* (New York: DeVinne Press, 1901), pp. 240-57. CtHi.

560. Hallowell, Henry. Pvt. Mass. "A Narrative of Henry Hallowell, of Lynn, Respecting the Revolution in 1775, 1776, 1777, 1778, 1779 to January 17, 1780." In Howard Kendall Sanderson, *Lynn in the Revolution*, pt. 1, pp. 149-83. Boston: W. B. Clarke, 1909.

561. Halsey, Zephaniah, and Ramsey, Archibald. Journal, New York, New Jersey, and Virginia, May 1779-Dec. 1782. *Pathfinder Magazine*, 8, 15, 22, 29 Sept. 1894.

562. Hamilton, Asa; Hamilton, William; and Hamilton, Joseph. Pvts. [?]. Mass. Journal, July 1776-Apr. 1795. Manuscript. 19 pp. DNA (Pension files).

563. Hand, Edward. Gen. Pa. Journal, Sullivan's expedition, 1779. Manuscript. NN.

564. Hanford, Levi. Pvt. Conn. In Charles I. Bushnell, *A Narrative of the Life and Adventures of Levi Hanford, a Soldier of the Revolution.* New York, 1863. 80 pp.

565. Hardenbergh, John L. Lt. N.Y. "Journal of Lieut. John L. Hardenbergh of the Second New York Continental Regiment from May 1 to October 3, 1779." Edited by John S. Clark. *Collections of the Cayuga County Historical Society* 1 (1879): 23-59. Reprinted in New York (State) Secretary of State, *Journals of the Military Expedition of Major General John Sullivan* (Auburn, 1887), pp. 115-36.

566. Hardy, Joseph. Capt. "Private Journal on Board the *Confederacy* Frigate Kept by Captain Joseph Hardy in Command of Marines [Dec. 1779-Feb. 1781]." In James L. Howard, *Seth Harding, Mariner: A Naval Picture of the Revolution*, pp. 213-77. New Haven: Yale

University Press, 1930. Also in Charles R. Smith, *Marines in the Revolution* (Washington, D.C.: Government Printing Office, 1975), pp. 359–76.

567. Harmar, Josiah. Gen. Pa. "Lieut. Colonel Josiah Harmar's Journal: No. 1, Commencing November 11th 1778." Manuscript. MiU-C.

568. ———. Diary, Aug. 1783–99. Manuscript. MiU-C.

569. Harris, Samuel, Jr. Journal, 1777–80. Manuscript. MH.

570. Hart, Aaron. Pvt. Conn. Journal and account book, June–Nov. 1783. Manuscript. 8 pp. DNA (Pension files).

571. Haskell, Caleb. Pvt. Mass. *Caleb Haskell's Diary, May 5, 1775–May 30, 1776: A Revolutionary Soldier's Record before Boston and with Arnold's Quebec Expedition.* Ed. by Lothrop Withington. Newburyport, Mass., 1881. 23 pp. Reprinted in *Magazine of History*, extra no. 86. Also in Kenneth Roberts, ed., *March to Quebec* (New York: Doubleday, Doran & Co., 1938), pp. 459–99.

572. Hatter, John. "Memorandums on Board of the Sloop *Commerce*." In R. W. Gibbes, *Documentary History of the American Revolution . . . 1764–1776*, pp. 121–23. New York, 1855. SCAr.

573. Hawkins, Christopher. Privateer. R.I. *The Adventures of Christopher Hawkins . . . in the Revolutionary War.* Edited by Charles I. Bushnell. New York, 1864. 316 pp. Reprint ed., New York: Arno Press, 1968.

574. Hawkins, John. Sgt. Maj. Pa. Journal, Jan. 1779–Dec. 1782. Manuscript. PHi.

575. Haws, Samuel. Minuteman. Mass. "A Journal for 1775 [Apr. 1775–Feb. 1776]." In Abraham Tomlinson, ed., *The Military Journals of Two Private Soldiers 1758–1775*, pp. 49–90. Poughkeepsie, N.Y., 1855.

576. Heart, Jonathan. Capt. Conn. Journal. Manuscript. OClWHi.

577. Heath, William. Maj. Gen. Mass. *Memoirs of Major-General Heath; Containing Anecdotes, Details of Skirmishes, Battles, and Other Military Events during the American War.* Boston, 1798. 388 pp. Reprint ed., New York: Arno Press, 1968. Reprint ed., Freeport, N.Y.: Books for Libraries Press, 1970.

578. Hempstead, Stephen. Sgt. Conn. *See* 740.

579. Hendricks, William, Capt. Pa.; and John Chambers, Capt. [Pvt.], Pa. "Journal of Captain William Hendricks from Carlisle to Boston, Thence to Quebec, 1775." Reprint of an anonymous pamphlet, *A Journal of the March of a Party of Provincials from Carlisle*

to Boston, and From Thence to Quebec, Begun the 13th of July and Ended the 31st of December, 1775 (Glasglow, 1776) in *Pennsylvania Archives*, 2d ser. 15: 21-58. [Justin H. Smith, *Arnold's March from Cambridge to Quebec* (New York: G. P. Putnam, 1938), pp. 39-40, and Kenneth Roberts, ed., *March to Quebec* (New York: Doubleday, Doran & Co., 1938), p. xiii, argue that this journal was written by Sgt. William McCoy.]

580. Henry, John Joseph. Pvt. Pa. *An Accurate and Interesting Account of the Hardships and Sufferings of That Band of Heroes, Who Traversed the Wilderness in the Campaign against Quebec in 1775.* Lancaster, Pa., 1812. 221 pp. Reprinted as *Account of Arnold's Campaign against Quebec* (Albany, 1877). Reprint ed., New York: Arno Press, 1968. Also in *Pennsylvania Archives*, 2d ser. 15:59-191. Also in Kenneth Roberts, ed., *March to Quebec* (New York:Doubleday, Doran & Co., 1938), pp. 299-429. PHi.

581. Herbert, Charles. Seaman. Mass. *A Relic of the Revolution, Containing a Full and Particular Account of the Sufferings and Privations of All the American Prisoners Captured on the High Seas, and Carried into Plymouth, England, during the Revolution of 1776.* Boston, 1847. 258 pp. Reprint ed., New York: Arno Press, 1968.

582. Herttell, Thomas. *See* 740.

583. Heth, William. Lt. Va. [?]. Prison journal at Quebec, Feb.-July 1776. *Annual Papers of the Winchester Historical Society* 1 (1931): 27-118. DLC.

584. Hildreth, Micah. Lt. Mass. Journal, march to Ticonderoga, Aug.-Oct. 1776. In Silas R. Coburn, *History of Dracut, Massachusetts*, pp. 147-52. Lowell, Mass.: Courier-Citizen Co., 1922.

585. Hill, Baylor. Capt. [?]. Va. [?]. Journal, 1777-80. Manuscript. CSmH.

586. Hill, Jonathan. Diary, expedition to Quebec, Apr.-May 1776. Manuscript. MHi.

587. Hill, William. Col. *Col. William Hill's Memoirs of the Revolution.* Edited by A. S. Salley, Jr. Columbia: The Historical Commission of South Carolina, 1921. 36 pp. DLC (copy) .

588. Hitchcock, Enos. Chaplain. R.I. "Diary of Enos Hitchcock, D.D.: A Chaplain in the Revolutionary Army [Apr. 1777-Aug. 1779]." Edited by William B. Weeden. *Publications of the Rhode Island Historical Society*, n.s. 7 (1899-1900):87-134, 147-94, 207-31.

589. Holland, Park. Lt. Mass. Autobiography in the form of a letter

covering his life to the end of the Revolution. Manuscript. MeBaHi (copy).

590. Hollister, Josiah. Pvt. [?]. Conn. *The Journal of Josiah Hollister, a Soldier of the American Revolution and A Prisoner of War in Canada.* Chicago [?]: privately printed, 1928. 43 pp.

591. How, David. Pvt. Mass. *Diary of David How, a Private in Colonel Paul Dudley Sargent's Regiment of the Massachusetts Line, in the Army of the American Revolution, [Dec. 1775-Nov. 1777].* Edited by George Wingate Chase and Henry B. Dawson. Morrisania, N.Y., 1865. 51 pp.

592. Howe, Estes. Surgeon. Mass. Journal, Saratoga campaign, 1777-78. Manuscript. NN.

593. Hubley, Adam. Lt. Col. Pa. "Adm. Hubley, Jr., Lt. Colo. Comdt. 11th Penna Regt., His Journal, Commencing at Wyoming, July 30th, 1779." *Pennsylvania Magazine of History and Biography* 33 (1909): 129-46, 279-302, 409-22. Also in Charles Miner, *History of Wyoming* (Philadelphia, 1845), app., pp. 81-104. Reprinted in New York (State) Secretary of State, *Journals of the Military Expedition of Major General John Sullivan* (Auburn, 1887), pp. 145-67. DLC.

594. Hughes, James M. Lt. N.Y. "Notes Relative to the Campaign against Burgoyne [1777]." *Proceedings of the Massachusetts Historical Society* 3 (1855-58):278-80.

595. Hull, William. Maj. Mass. "Capture of Stony Point, July, 1779: From Manuscript in the Possession of His Grandson." *Magazine of American History* 28 (1892):182-85.

596. Humphrey, William. Lt. R.I. "A Journal Kept by William Humphrey of Capt. Thayer's Company, on a March to Quebec ... [Sept.] 1775-[Aug.] 1776." *Magazine of History*, extra no. 166. RHi.

597. Ingalls, Phineas. Pvt. Mass. "Revolutionary War Journal, Kept by Phineas Ingalls of Andover, Mass., April 19, 1775-December 8, 1776." *Historical Collections of the Essex Institute* 53 (1917):81-92.

598. Irvine, William. Gen. Pa. "Gen. Irvine's Journal of the Canadian Campaign, [May] 1776." *Historical Magazine* 6 (1862):115-17.

599. "Itinerary of the Pennsylvania Line from Pennsylvania to South Carolina, [May] 1781-[July] 1782." *Pennsylvania Magazine of History and Biography* 36 (1912):273-92.

600. Jackson, Matthew. Pvt. Conn. Family record book of Jane Jackson. Manuscript. 21 pp. DNA (Pension files).

601. Jamison, John. Capt. Journal, Oct. 1776-Dec. 1779. *American Monthly Magazine* 23 (1903):12-13.

602. Jenkins, John. Lt. Conn. "Journal of Lieut. John Jenkins [Apr.-Dec. 1779]." In New York (State) Secretary of State, *Journals of the Military Expedition of Major General John Sullivan,* pp. 169-77. Auburn, 1887.

603. Jennison, William. Lt. Mass. "Journal of William Jennison, Lieutenant of Marines." In Charles R. Smith, *Marines in the Revolution,* pp. 343-57. Washington, D.C.: Government Printing Office, 1975. Extracts in *Pennsylvania Magazine of History and Biography* 15 (1891):101-8. DLC, PHi.

604. Johnson, Thomas. Col. Vt. Prison journal, Mar.-Oct. 1781. In Frederick P. Wells, *History of Newbury, Vermont, from the Discovery of the Coös Country to Present Time, with Genealogical Records of Many Families,* pp. 384-93. St. Johnsbury, Vt.: Caledonian Co., 1902.

605. Joslin, Joseph, Jr. Teamster. Conn. "Journal of Joseph Joslin, Jr., of South Killingly, a Teamster in the Continental Service, March 1777-August 1778." *Collections of the Connecticut Historical Society* 7 (1899):297-369.

606. Journal by an officer at Fort Stanwix, 1777. Manuscript. DLC.

607. Journal by participants in Williamson's campaign against the Cherokees. Manuscript. WHi.

608. Journal, Mar. 1777-Aug. 1778. Manuscript. MSaE.

609. Journal of a Connecticut soldier, New Jersey, 1780. Manuscript. DLC.

610. "Journal of a Cruise in 1777 in the Privateer Brig *Oliver Cromwell,* [July-Nov. 1777]." *Historical Collections of the Essex Institute* 45 (1909): 245-55.

611. "Journal of a Pennsylvania Soldier, July-December, 1776." *Bulletin of the New York Public Library* 8 (1904):547-49.

612. "Journal of a Revolutionary Soldier [Pvt.] in [July-Dec.] 1776." *Historical Magazine* 7 (1863):366-68.

613. Journal of Montgomery's Canadian expedition, 1775. Manuscript. NHi.

614. Journal of Saratoga campaign, 1777. Manuscript. MH.

615. Journal of Sullivan's expedition, May-Oct. 1779. Manuscript. 84 pp. DLC (Force transcripts).

616. Journal of Sullivan's expedition, 1779. *Hill's New Hampshire Patriot,* 16 Sept. 1843.

617. "Journal of the March of Gen. Clinton's Brigade from Albany to Tioga in the Susquehanna [June-Aug. 1779]." Manuscript. MWA (copy?).

618. "Journal of the Siege of York in Virginia by a Chaplain in the American Army [Sept-Oct. 1781]." *Collections of the Massachusetts Historical Society* 9 (1804):102-8.

619. "Journal of the Siege of York in Virginia [by a French Engineer, Sept.-Oct. 1781]." *Magazine of American History* 4 (1880):449-52.

620. Journal, Rhode Island, Aug. 1780. Manuscript. MBNEH.

621. Journal, Rhode Island, 1780. Manuscript. MSaE.

622. Journals of officers in Sullivan's expedition, 1779. Manuscript. NHi, NCanHi (copy).

623. Kettel, Andrew. Sgt. Maj. Mass. Journal, Apr. 1780-May 1781. Manuscript. 68 pp. DNA (Pension files).

624. Kettell, John. Pvt. Mass. Journal, siege of Boston, Bunker Hill, May-Oct. 1775. Manuscript. MHi.

625. Kimball, Daniel. Ens. N.H. Journal, march to Quebec, Feb.-May 1776. Manuscript. 27 pp. DNA (Pension files).

626. Kimball, M. *See* 680.

627. Kimball, Peter. Capt. N.H. "Diary of Capt. Peter Kimball, [Sept.-Dec.] 1776." Edited by Charles Carleton Coffin. *The Granite Monthly* 4 (1881):230-33.

628. ———. Journal, July-Sept. 1777. In Charles Carleton Coffin, *The History of Boscawen and Webster [N.H.] from 1733 to 1878*, pp. 261-64. Concord, N.H., 1878.

629. Kirkwood, Robert. Capt. Del. "The Journal and Order Book of Captain Robert Kirkwood of the Delaware Regiment of the Continental Line." Pt. 1, "A Journal of the Southern Campaign [Apr. 1780-Apr. 1782]." Edited by Joseph Brown Turner, *Papers of the Delaware Historical Society* 56 (1910): 9-30. Reprint ed., Port Washington, N.Y.: Kennikat Press, 1970. DLC (Force transcripts), MH.

630. Knox, Henry. Maj. Gen. Mass. "Knox's Diary during His Ticonderoga Expedition [Nov. 1775-Jan. 1776]." *New England Historical and Genealogical Register* 30 (1876):321-26. MBNEH.

631. Krafft, John Charles Philip von. Lt. Prussia. "Journal of Lt. John Charles Philip von Krafft, 1776-1784." *Collections of the New-York Historical Society* 15 (1882): 1-200. [Krafft spent short periods on an American privateer and in American camp while soliciting a commission.]

632. Lacey, John. Brig. Gen. Pa. "Memoirs of Brigadier-General John Lacey, of Pennsylvania [1775-Dec. 1777]." *Pennsylvania Magazine of History and Biography* 25 (1901): 1-13, 191-207, 341-54, 498-515; 26 (1902):101-11, 265-70. PHi.

633. Latham, Milton S. Officer. France. Journal, Apr. 1780-Mar. 1783. Manuscript. DLC.

634. Lauzun, Duc de. Brig. Gen. France. *See* 387.

635. Lawson, Thomas. Capt. Conn. Extracts from journal, Oct. 1777. In Charles Hammond, *The History of Union, Conn., Founded on Material Gathered by Rev. Charles Hammond*, compiled by Harvey M. Lawson, p. 125. New Haven, 1893.

636. Lee, Andrew. Capt. Pa. [?]. "Sullivan's Expedition to Staten Island in 1777: Extract from the Diary of Captain Andrew Lee." *Pennsylvania Magazine of History and Biography* 3 (1879):167-73.

637. Lee, Henry. Lt. Col. Va. *Memoirs of the War in the Southern Department of the United States*. Philadelphia and New York, 1812. 2 vols. 2d ed. (with revisions and a biography of the author by Robert E. Lee), New York, 1869. Reprint ed., New York: Arno Press, 1969.

638. Lee, Jesse. Chaplain. Va. In Minton Thrift, *Memoir of the Rev. Jesse Lee with Extracts from His Journals*, pp. 25-35, *passim* (for journal excerpts). New York, 1823.

639. Leggett, Abraham. Ens. N.Y. *The Narrative of Major Abraham Leggett, of the Army of the Revolution*. Edited by Charles I. Bushnell. New York, 1865. 72 pp. Reprint ed., New York: Arno Press, 1971.

640. Lenoir, William. N.C. Journal, Aug.-Oct. 1776. *Journal of Southern History* 6 (1940):247-57.

641. Libby, Jonathan. Capt. Mass. Memoir, Mar. 1777-Apr. 1780. Manuscript. 12 pp. DNA (Pension files).

642. Lincoln, Benjamin. Maj. Gen. Mass. Journals, Oct.-Dec. 1778, Sept.-Oct. 1779. Manuscript. DLC, NN.

643. Lincoln, Rufus. Capt. Mass. *The Papers of Captain Rufus Lincoln, of Wareham, Mass.* Edited by James Minor Lincoln. Cambridge, Mass.: Riverside Press, 1904. 274 pp. Reprint ed., New York: Arno Press, 1971.

644. [Litchfield, Paul]. Pvt. Mass. Extracts from diary, Mar. 1775-July 1775. *Proceedings of the Massachusetts Historical Society* 19 (1881-82):376-79. MHi.

645. Little, Moses. Col. Mass. [?]. Diary, 1776-1814. Manuscript. MeHi.

646. Livermore, Daniel. Capt. N.H. "A Journal of the March of Gen. Poor's Brigade ... May 17 [to Dec.] 1779." *Collections of the New Hampshire Historical Society* 6 (1850):308-35. Also in New York (State) Secretary of State, *Journals of the Military Expedition of*

Major General John Sullivan (Auburn, 1887), pp. 178-91. DLC (Force transcripts). [Manuscript journal includes additional entries for 1780 and 1782.]

647. Livingston, Henry. Maj. N.Y. "Journal of Major Henry Livingston, of the Third New York Continental Line, August to December 1775." Edited by Gaillard Hunt. *Pennsylvania Magazine of History and Biography* 22 (1898):9-33. NN.

648. Lock, Benjamin. Pvt. Mss. Travel log, Oct.-Nov. 1777. Manuscript. 8 pp. DNA (Pension files).

649. Long, Enoch. Cpl. N.H. Journal, July 1779-Dec. 1780. Manuscript. 30 pp. DNA (Pension files).

650. Lovell, Solomon. Gen. Mass. Journal, Penobscot expedition, July-Aug. 1779. *Publications of the Weymouth Historical Society* 1 (1881):95-105.

651. Loxley, Benjamin. Capt. Pa. "A Journal of the Campaign to Amboy, and Other Parts of the Jerseys [July-Aug. 1776]." *Collections of the Historical Society of Pennsylvania* 1 (1853):223-36. PHi.

652. Lunt, Paul. Mass. *Paul Lunt's Diary, May-December 1775.* Edited by Samuel A. Green. Boston, 1872. 19 pp. Also in *Proceedings of the Massachusetts Historical Society* 12 (1871-73):192-206.

653. Lyman, Daniel. Maj. Mass. Journal, 1780. Manuscript. RHi.

654. Lyman, Joseph. Chaplain [?]. Journal, Saratoga campaign, 1777. Manuscript. MBC.

655. Lyman, Simeon. Pvt. Conn. "Journal of Simeon Lyman of Sharon, Aug. 10 to Dec. 28, 1775." *Collections of the Connecticut Historical Society* 7 (1899):98, 111-34.

656. ———. Journal, New York and New Jersey, Aug. 1776-Jan. 1777. Manuscript. 37 pp. DNA (Pension files).

657. ———. Journal, Connecticut, Sept.-Dec. 1777. Manuscript. 15 pp. DNA (Pension files).

658. MacArthur, Charles. Surgeon. Pa. Journal, Sullivan's expedition, 1779. Manuscript. PPL (copy).

659. McClellan, Joseph. Capt. Pa. "Diary of the Revolt in the Pennsylvania Line, January, 1781." In John Blair Linn and William H. Egle, eds., *Pennsylvania in the War of the Revolution, Battalions and Line, 1775-1783*, 2:631-74. *Pennsylvania Archives*, 2d ser., vol. 11. Harrisburg, 1880.

660. ———. Extract from journal, Feb.-May 1781. In John Blair Linn and William H. Egle, eds., *Pennsylvania in the War of the Revolution, Battalions and Line, 1775-1783*, 1:396-97. *Pennsylvania Archives*, 2d ser., vol. 10. Harrisburg, 1880.

661. ———. "Diary of the Pennsylvania Line [May-June 1781]." In John Blair Linn and William H. Egle, eds., *Pennsylvania in the War of the Revolution, Battalions and Line, 1775-1783*, 2:677-78. *Pennsylvania Archives*, 2d ser., vol. 11. Harrisburg, 1880. [This diary continues through April 1782 (pp. 678-727) but after 13 June 1781 the diary is that of William Feltman. *See* 507.]

662. McCoy, William. Sgt. Pa. *See* 579.

663. McCready, Robert. Pvt. Pa. Journal, New York, Nov. 1776. Manuscript. DLC.

664. McCully, George. Ens. Pa. In Clarence M. Burton, "Epraim Douglas and His Times: A Fragment of History with the Journal of George McCully [July-Aug. 1783] (Hitherto Unpublished) and Various Letters of the Period." *Magazine of History*, extra no. 10. DLC.

665. McCurtin, Daniel. Pvt. Md. [?]. "Journal of the Times at the Siege of Boston since our Arrival at Cambridge, near Boston [July 1775-May 1776]." In Thomas Balch, ed., *Papers Relating Chiefly to the Maryland Line During the Revolution*, pp. 11-41. Publications of the Seventy-Six Society, vol. 4. Philadelphia, 1857.

666. McDowell, William. Lt. Pa. "Journal of Lieutenant McDowell of the First 'Penn'a Regiment,' in the Southern Campaign, [May] 1781-[Dec.] 1782." *Pennsylvania Archives*, 2d ser. 15:297-340.

667. McHenry, James. Maj. Md. *Journal of a March, a Battle, and a Waterfall; Being the Version Elaborated by James McHenry from His Diary of the Year 1778; Begun at Valley Forge, and Containing Accounts of the British, the Indians, and the Battle of Monmouth.* N.p.: privately printed, 1945. 11 pp. MiU-C, NN.

668. Machin, Thomas. Capt. N.Y. "Journal of March from Fort Schuyler: Expedition against the Onondagas, 1779." *Magazine of History* 3, pt. 2 (1879):688-89. Reprinted in New York (State) Secretary of State, *Journals of the Military Expeditions of Major General John Sullivan* (Auburn, 1887), pp. 192-95.

669. McKendry, William. Lt. Mass. Journal of William McKendry, Oct. 1777-Jan. 1780. *Proceedings of the Massachusetts Historical Society*, 2d ser. 2 (1885-86):442-78. Extract in New York (State) Secretary of State, *Journals of the Military Expedition of Major General John Sullivan* (Auburn, 1887), pp. 198-212.

670. McMichael, James. Lt. Pa. "Diary of Lieutenant James McMichael, of the Pennsylvania Line, [May] 1776-[May] 1778." *Pennsylvania Magazine of History and Biography* 16 (1892):129-59. Also in *Pennsylvania Archives*, 2d ser. 15:195-218.

671. McNeill, Samuel. Quartermaster. Pa. "Journal of Samuel McNeill, B.Q.M.; 'His Orderly Book' [Aug.-Sept.] 1779." *Pennsylvania Archives*, 2d ser. 15:753-59. [Despite the title, part of this work is a diary.] NHi.

672. McPherson [MacPherson?], William. Lt. Pa. [?]. "Extract from the Journal of Lieut. William McPherson [Aug.-Nov. 1776]." *Memoirs of the Long Island Historical Society* 3, pt. 2 (1878):168-69.

673. McQueen, Joshua. Journal, 1779-82. Manuscript. MoU.

674. Martin, Joseph Plumb. Pvt. Conn. *A Narrative of Some of the Adventures, Dangers and Sufferings of a Revolutionary Soldier.* Hallowell, Me., 1830. 213 pp. Also, George F. Scheer, ed., *Private Yankee Doodle: Being a Narrative ...* (Boston: Little, Brown, 1962). Reprint ed., New York: Arno Press, 1968.

675. Matthewman, Luke. Lt. "Narrative of Lieut. Luke Matthewman of the Revolutionary Navy [Mar. 1776-1783?]." *Magazine of American History* 2, pt. 1 (1878):175-85.

676. Maxwell, Hugh. Mass. *The Christian Patriot: Some Recollections of the Late Col. Hugh Maxwell, of Massachusetts.* New York, 1833. 139 pp.

677. Maxwell, Thompson. Lt. N.H. "The Narrative of Major Thompson Maxwell; Compiled from Manuscripts ... Written out from His Dictation in 1818 [1757-1814]." *Historical Collections of Essex Institute* 7 (1865): 97-116. MSaE.

678. Medbury, John. Lt. Mass. [?]. Journal, 1776. Manuscript. RHi.

679. Meigs, Return Jonathan. Maj. Conn. "A Journal of Occurrences ... in the Detachment Commanded by Col. Benedict Arnold [Sept. 1775-Jan. 1776]." *Collections of the Massachusetts Historical Society*, 2d ser. 2 (1814):227-47. Also in Kenneth Roberts, ed., *March to Quebec* (New York: Doubleday, Doran & Co., 1938), pp. 171-92.

680. Melvin, James. Pvt. Mass. *Journal of the Expedition to Quebec, in the year 1775, under the command of Colonel Benedict Arnold.* Philadelphia, 1864. 34 pp. Reprinted in Kenneth Roberts, ed., *March to Quebec* (New York: Doubleday, Doran & Co., 1938), pp. 433-54. [Roberts believes this journal is an elaboration of one by M. Kimball, which is privately owned and unpublished.]

681. Menonville, Louis Antoine Thiebault de. Maj. France. "Journal of the Siege of York [Oct. 1781]." *Magazine of American History* 7 (1881):283-88.

682. Merriam, Joseph. Diary, 1772-87. Manuscript. MB.

683. Merrick, Samuel F. Pvt. Mass. Journal, Saratoga, Sept.-Oct. 1777. In Chauncey E. Peck, *The History of Wilbraham, Massachusetts*, pp. 136-38. Wilbraham [?], Mass., 1914. Also in Rufus P. Stebbins, *An Historical Address, Delivered at the Centennial Celebration of the Incorporation of the Town of Wilbraham* (Boston, 1864), pp. 238-40.

684. Miles, Samuel. Col. Pa. "Journal of Col. Samuel Miles, Concerning the Battle of Long Island — 1776." *Pennsylvania Archives*, 2d ser. 1:519-22. DLC.

685. Mills, Zachariah. Lt. Va. Receipt book including a brief description of a march from Richmond to Yorktown, Jan.-Aug. 1781. Manuscript. 15 pp. DNA (Pension files).

686. Moody, William. Drummer. Mass. "William Moody's Journal, [July-Aug. 1779]." *Collections and Proceedings of the Maine Historical Society*, 2d ser. 10 (1899):144-48.

687. More, Charles Albert. France. *A French Volunteer of the War of Independence (the Chevalier de Pontgibaud)*. Translated and edited by Robert B. Douglas. New York, 1897. Reprint ed., New York: B. Blom, 1972. 2d ed., Paris, 1898. Reprint ed., New York: Arno Press, 1969.

688. Morgan, Nathaniel. "Journal of Ensign Nathaniel Morgan, April 21 to Dec. 11, 1775: Items of the Siege of Boston from the Roxbury Side." *Collections of the Connecticut Historical Society* 7 (1899):99, 101-10.

689. Morison, George. Pvt. Pa. *An Interesting Journal of Occurrences during the Expedition to Quebec*. Hagerstown, Md., 1803. 66 pp. Reprinted in *Magazine of History*, extra no. 52. Also in Kenneth Roberts, ed., *March to Quebec* (New York: Doubleday, Doran & Co., 1938), pp. 503-39. PHi, MH (copy).

690. Morris, James. Capt. Conn. Memoir, 1776-82. Manuscript. 20 pp. DNA (Pension files).

691. Morsman, Oliver. Pvt. Mass. *A History of Breed's (Commonly Called) Bunker's Hill Battle, Fought between the Provincial Troops and the British, June 17, 1775*. Sackett's Harbor, N.Y., 1830. 17 pp. [Possibly an eyewitness account.]

692. Mott, Edward. Capt. Conn. "Journal of Capt. Edward Mott [Apr.-May, 1775]." *Collections of the Connecticut Historical Society* 1:163-74.

693. Moultrie, William. Maj. Gen. S.C. *Memoirs of the American Revolution, So Far As It Related to the States of North and South*

Carolina, and Georgia. New York, 1802. 2 vols. Reprint ed., New York: Arno Press, 1968.

694. Mountjoy, Alvin. Lt. Va. Journal, New York, Sept.-Oct. 1775. Manuscript. 4 pp. DNA (Pension files).

695. Mudge, Simon. Mass. Journal, Ticonderoga, July-Nov. 1776. *Collections of the Danvers Historical Society* 27 (1939):40-43. Also in Alfred Mudge, *To the Mudge Family* ... (Boston[?], 1865[?]), pp. 204-5.

696. Myddelton [Middleton?], Charles S. Capt. S.C. "Journal of Captain Charles S. Middleton [Dec. 1776-Jan. 1777]." In R. W. Gibbes, *Documentary History of the American Revolution ... 1776-1782*, pp. 47-54. New York, 1857.

697. Nash, Solomon. Pvt. Mass. *Journal of Solomon Nash; a Soldier of the Revolution, [Jan.] 1776-[Jan.] 1777.* Edited by Charles I. Bushnell. New York, 1861. 46 pp. NHi.

698. Nelson, George. Journal, 1780-81. Manuscript. PHi.

699. *The Never Was Is Not nor Never Shall Be; or, A Narrative of the Travels of an Old Revolutionary Soldier Who Traveled through the War under the Command of Our Mild Hero Washington.* N.p., ca. 1818. 16 pp.

700. Newell, James. Capt. "Orderly Book and Journal of James Newell during the Point Pleasant Campaign, [Sept.-Oct.] 1774." *Virginia Magazine of History and Biography* 11 (1903-4):242-53.

701. Nice, John. Capt. Pa. "Extracts from the Diary of Captain John Nice [Aug.-Dec. 1776, Jan.-June 1778]." *Pennsylvania Magazine of History and Biography* 16 (1892):399-411. PHi.

702. Nichols, Francis. Lt. Pa. "Diary of Lieutenant Francis Nichols of Colonel William Thompson's Battalion of Pennsylvania Riflemen, January to September, 1776." *Pennsylvania Magazine of History and Biography* 20 (1896):504-14.

703. Norris, James. Capt. Journal, Sullivan's expedition, June-Oct. 1779. *Publications of the Buffalo Historical Society* 1 (1879):217-52. Reprinted, with revisions, in New York (State) Secretary of State, *Journals of the Military Expedition of Major General John Sullivan* (Auburn, 1887), pp. 223-39. NBuHi, NN, WHi.

704. Norton, George. Pvt. [?]. Mass. "Revolutionary Diary Kept by George Norton of Ipswich, 1777-1778." *Historical Collections of the Essex Institute* 74 (1938):337-49.

705. Nukerck, Charles. Lt. N.Y. "Journal of Lieut. Charles Nukerck [May 1779-Dec. 1780]." In New York (State) Secretary of State,

Journals of the Military Expedition of Major General John Sullivan, pp. 213-22. Auburn, 1887.

706. Nutting, William. Cpl. Mass. Diary, 1777-1804. Manuscript. MHi.

707. O'Connor, M. Officer. France. "Journal du siège de Savannah: Avec des observations de M. le Comte D'Estaing [Sept.-Oct. 1779]." Manuscript. MiU-C (copy).

708. Ogden, Aaron. Paymaster. N.J. *Autobiography of Col. Aaron Ogden, of Elizabethtown.* Patterson, 1893. 33 pp. Also in *Proceedings of the New Jersey Historical Society*, 2d ser. 12 (1892-93):13-31.

709. Ogden, Matthias. N.J. "Journal of Major Matthias Ogden [Oct.-Nov.] 1775." *Proceedings of the New Jersey Historical Society*, n.s. 13 (1928):17-30.

710. "Operations in Maine in [July-Aug.] 1779: Journal Found on Board the *Hunter*, Continental Ship of Eighteen Guns." *Historical Magazine* 8 (1864):51-54.

711. Oswald, Eleazer. Capt. Conn. "A Journal of an Intended Tour from Cambridge to Quebec, via Kennebec, with a Detachment of Two Regiments of Musketeers and Three Companies of Riflers, Consisting of About Eleven Hundred Effective Men, Commanded by Benedict Arnold, [Sept.-Oct. 1775]." In Peter Force, ed., *American Archives*, 4th ser. 3:1058-62. [Sometimes referred to as the "missing first pages of Arnold's journal." It is written in the first person as if Arnold were writing, but Justin H. Smith, *Arnold's March from Cambridge to Quebec* (New York: G.P. Putnam, 1938), p. 264, states "it is best to speak of the journal as Oswald's."]

712. Paine, Samuel. Scout. N.H. [?]. "Diary of Travel on a Scouting Party [July-Aug. 1776]." *Provincial and State Papers of New Hampshire* 17:72.

713. Painter, Thomas. Pvt. [?]. Conn. [?]. *Autobiography of Thomas Painter, Relating His Experience during the War of the Revolution* [1776-83?]. Washington, D.C. [?]: privately printed, 1910. 106 pp.

714. Parker, Benjamin. Ens. Me. Journal, New York, Dec. 1776-Mar. 1777. *Old Eliot: A Quarterly Magazine of History and Biography* 6 (1903):148-51.

715. Parker, James. Pvt. [?]. Mass. "Extracts from the Diary of James Parker of Shirley, Mass. [Jan. 1770-Dec. 1829]." *New England Historical and Genealogical Register* 69 (1915):8-17, 117-27, 211-24, 294-308; 70 (1916):9-24, 137-46, 210-20, 294-308.

716. Parker, Nahum. Pvt. Mass. Journals, New England, New York, New Jersey, Apr. 1777–Dec. 1780. Manuscript. DNA (Pension files).

717. Parker, Robert. Lt. Pa. "Journal of Lieutenant Robert Parker of the Second Continental Artillery, [June–Dec.] 1779." *Pennsylvania Magazine of History and Biography* 27 (1903):404–20; 28 (1904): 12–25. Reprinted in New York (State) Division of Archives and History, *The Sullivan-Clinton Campaign in 1779* (Albany, 1929), pp. 188–210.

718. Parkman, Ebenezer, Jr. Sgt. Mass. Diary, partly at Morristown, June 1779–Sept. 1793. Manuscript. MWA.

719. Pawling, Henry. Capt. N.Y. Prison ship journal, Oct. 1777–Feb. 1778. *Olde Ulster: An Historical and Genealogical Magazine* 1 (1905):335–38, 361–65; 2 (1906):18–25.

720. Peale, Charles Willson. Capt. Pa. "Journal by Charles Willson Peale [Dec. 1776–Jan. 1777]." *Pennsylvania Magazine of History and Biography* 38 (1914):271–86.

721. Pennington, William S. "Copy of Diary of William S. Pennington, of New Jersey (May 4, 1780–March 22, 1781)." *Journal of the Military Service Institute of the United States* 4 (1883):314–29. Also in *Proceedings of the New Jersey Historical Society*, n.s. 63 (1945):199; 64 (1946):42. NjHi.

722. Perry, David. Capt. [?]. Conn. *Recollections of an Old Soldier: The Life of Captain David Perry, a Soldier of the French and Revolutionary Wars; Containing Many Extraordinary Occurrences Relating to His Own Private History, and an Account of Some Interesting Events in the History of the Times in Which He Lived.* Windsor, Vt., 1882. 55 pp.

723. Perry, Ichabod Jeremiah. Pvt. Conn. *Reminiscences of the Revolution.* Lima, N.Y.: Ska-Hase-Ga-O Chapter, DAR, 1915. 63 pp.

724. Perry, Joseph. Chaplain [?]. Journal, 1776–77. Manuscript. GHi.

725. Phillips, Abraham. N.C. Journal, southern campaign, Sept.–Dec. 1781, June 1782–Feb. 1783. Manuscript. DLC.

726. Pickering, Timothy. Col. Mass. Extracts from journal. In Octavius Pickering, *The Life of Timothy Pickering*, vol. 1 *passim.* Boston, 1867. MSaE.

727. Pierce, John. Sgt. Mass. "Journal by the Advance Surveyor with Col. Arnold on the March to Quebec." In Kenneth Roberts, ed., *March to Quebec*, pp. 651–711. New York: Doubleday, Doran & Co., 1940.

728. Pierce, Samuel. Col. Mass. Extracts from diary. In Dorchester Antiquarian and Historical Society, *History of the Town of Dorchester*, pp. 358, 588. Boston, 1859.
729. Pierce, William. Capt. Va. Journal, Sullivan's expedition, 1779. Manuscript. PPL.
730. Pierpoint, Thomas. Pvt. [?]. Conn. Account book, including some material on revolutionary service, Dec. 1777–May 1782. Manuscript. DNA (Pension files).
731. Pitman, John. Extracts from diary, 1776–1822. In Alice Morse Earle, "A Baptist Preacher and Soldier of the Last Century." *New England Magazine* 18 (1895):407–14. RHi.
732. Pomeroy, Seth. Gen. Mass. Journal, Jan. 1777. In James Russell Trumbull, *History of Northampton [Mass.] from Its Settlement in 1654*, 2:121, 260. Northampton, Mass., 1902.
733. Porter, Elisha. Col. Mass. "The Diary of Colonel Elisha Porter, of Hadley, Massachusetts: Touching His March to the Relief of the Continental Forces before Quebec [Jan.–Aug. 1776]." *Magazine of American History* 30 (1893):185–206.
734. Porter, Jonathan. Pvt. [?]. Journal, Rhode Island, 1778. Manuscript. MSaE.
735. [Porterfield, Charles. Va.?] Diary of a prisoner at Quebec, Mar.–July 1776. *Publications of the Southern Historical Association* 6 (1902):113–31, 199 209, 295–303, 400–407. Extracts in *Virginia Magazine of History and Biography* 9 (1901-2):144–52. Extracts in *Magazine of American History* 21 (1889):318–19.
736. Potter, Israel Ralph. Pvt. [?]. R.I. *Life and Remarkable Adventures of Israel R. Potter, ... Who Was a Soldier in the American Revolution ... after Which He Was Taken Prisoner by the British, Conveyed to England, Where for Thirty Years He Obtained a Livelihood for Himself and Family*. Providence, 1824. 108 pp. Reprinted in *Magazine of History*, extra no. 16.
737. Potter, John. Capt. Mass. [?]. Journal, New York, 1778–79. Manuscript. N (copy).
738. Preble, Jedidiah. Brig. Gen. Mass. Journal, Aug. 1775–Nov. 1782. In George Henry Preble, *Genealogical Sketch of the First Three Generations of Prebles in America*, pp. 61–91 Boston, 1868. MBNEH.
739. Ramsey, Archibald. *See* 561.
740. Rathbun, Jonathan. Pvt. [?]. Conn. *Narrative of Jonathan Rath-*

bun, with Accurate Accounts of the Capture of Groton Fort, the Massacre That Followed, and the Sacking and Burning of New London, September 6, 1781 ... [with narratives] by Rufus Avery and Stephen Hempstead, Eyewitnesses of the Same. New London [?], 1840. 80 pp. Reprinted, with the additional narrative of Thomas Herttell, in *Magazine of History*, extra no. 15. Reprint ed., New York: Arno Press, 1971.

741. Redfield, Levi. Pvt. [?]. Conn. *A Succinct Account of Some Memorable Events and Occurrences in the Life of Levi Redfield, Late of Connecticut, Now Residing in Brattleboro, Ver.* Brattleborough, Vt., 1798. 12 pp.

742. Reed, Joseph. Col. Pa. "General Joseph Reed's Narrative of the Movements of the American Army in the Neighborhood of Trenton in the Winter of 1776-77." *Pennsylvania Magazine of History and Biography* 8 (1884):391-402.

743. Reidhead, William. Me. Journal, siege of Majabiguaduce, July-Aug. 1779. *Bangor Historical Magazine* 5 (1889-90):226-31.

744. Richards, Samuel. Capt. Conn. *Diary of Samuel Richards, Captain of Connecticut Line, War of Revolution, 1775-1781.* Philadelphia: privately printed, 1909. 117 pp.

745. Ritter, Jacob. Pvt. Pa. *Memoirs of Jacob Ritter, a Faithful Minister in the Society of Friends.* Edited by Joseph Foulke. Philadelphia, 1844. 118 pp.

746. Ritzema, Rudolphus. Col. (turncoat). N.Y. "Journal of Col. Rudolphus Ritzema of the First New York Regiment; August 8, 1775 to March 30, 1776." *Magazine of American History* 1, pt. 1 (1877): 98-107. NHi.

747. Robbins, Ammi Ruhamah. Chaplain. Conn. *Journal of the Rev. Ammi R. Robbins, a Chaplain in the American Army, in the Northern Campaign of 1776.* New Haven, 1850. 48 pp.

748. Roberts, Algernon. Lt. Pa. "A Journal of a Campaign from Philadelphia to Paulus Hook, [Aug.-Sept. 1776]." *Pennsylvania Magazine of History and Biography* 7 (1883):456-63. MH (Sparks manuscripts).

749. Roberts, James. *The Narrative of James Roberts, Soldier in the Revolutionary War and at the Battle of New Orleans.* Hattiesburg, Miss., 1858. 32 pp.

750. Roberts, Lemuel. Capt. [?]. Conn. *Memoirs of Captain Lemuel Roberts; Containing Adventures in Youth, Vicissitudes Experienced as a Continental Soldier, His Sufferings as a Prisoner, and Escapes*

from Captivity. Bennington, Vt., 1809. 96 pp. Reprint ed., New York: Arno Press, 1969.

751. Roberts, Thomas. Sgt. N.J. "Journal of Sergeant Thomas Roberts, [May–Sept. 1779]." In New York (State) Secretary of State, *Journals of the Military Expedition of Major General John Sullivan*, pp. 240–45. Auburn, 1887. NHi.

752. Robin, Abbe. Chaplain. France. *New Travels through North America.* Philadelphia, 1783. 112 pp. Reprint ed., New York: Arno Press, 1969.

753. Rochambeau, Jean Baptiste, Comte de. Lt. Gen. France. *Memoirs of the Marshal Count de Rochambeau, Relative to the War of Independence of the United States.* Translated by M.W.E. Wright. Paris, 1838. 114 pp. Reprint ed., New York: Arno Press, 1971. DLC.

754. Rochester, Nathaniel. Lt. Col. N.C. "Autobiography of Nathaniel Rochester, [1775–81]." In Galliard Hunt, ed., *Fragments of Revolutionary History*, pp. 99–105. Brooklyn, 1892.

755. Rodney, Thomas. Capt. Del. "Diary of Captain Thomas Rodney, [Dec.] 1776–[Jan.] 1777." *Papers of the Delaware Historical Society*, no. 8 (1888). 53 pp. Reprint ed., New York: DaCapo Press, 1974.

756. Rogers, William. Chaplain. Pa. *The Journal of a Brigade Chaplain in the Campaign of 1779 against the Six Nations under Command of Major-General John Sullivan.* Rhode Island Historical Tracts no. 7. Providence, 1879. 133 pp. Also in *Pennsylvania Archives*, 2d ser. 15:257–88; also in New York (State) Secretary of State, *Journals of the Military Expedition of Major General John Sullivan* (Auburn, 1887), pp. 246–65.

757. Rogers, William. Sgt. N.Y. "Journal of Sergeant William Rogers." In New York (State) Secretary of State, *Journals of the Military Expedition of Major General John Sullivan*, p. 266. Auburn, 1887.

758. Rosenthal, Gustavus de, Baron ("John Rose"). Maj. Russia. "Journal of a Volunteer Expedition to Sandusky, from May 24 to June 13, 1782." *Pennsylvania Magazine of History and Biography* 18 (1894): 129–57, 293–328. Reprint ed., New York: Arno Press, 1969.

759. Roundey, Joseph. Pvt. Mass. Journals, New England and New York, Mar. 1776–Jan. 1777. Manuscript. 31 pp. DNA (Pension files).

760. Russell, William. Maj. Mass. Prison diary, Dec. 1779–Aug. 1782. In Ralph D. Paine, *The Ships and Sailors of Old Salem*, pp. 124–74. New York: Outing Publishing Co., 1909.

761. Sanderson, Reuben. Lt. Conn. "Diary of the March from the Hud-

son to Yorktown, and Return, [July–Dec. 1781]." In Henry P. Johnston, *The Yorktown Campaign and the Surrender of Cornwallis, 1781*, pp. 170–73. New York, 1881. NNPM. [Manuscript diary covers 1775–1815.]

762. Sanger, Abner. Pvt. N.H. Journal extract. *Repertory*, vols. 1–2 (1924–27). DLC. [Manuscript journal covers Oct. 1774–Dec. 1782.]

763. Sawyer, Ebenezer. Journal, march to West Point, 1778–79. Manuscript. NN.

764. Scott, Robert. Pvt. [?]. Va. Journal, Feb. 1776–Oct. 1785. Manuscript. 15 pp. DNA (Pension files).

765. Scudder, William. N.J. *The Journal of William Scudder.* N.p., 1794. 250 pp. ["The only known copy is imperfect." Clifford K. Shipton and James E. Mooney, *National Index of American Imprints through 1800: The Short Title Evans*, Evans no. 27681.]

766. Segar, Nathaniel. Lt. Mass. *A Brief Narrative of the Captivity and Sufferings of Lt. Nathan'l. Segar, Who Was Taken Prisoner by the Indians and Carried to Canada, during the Revolutionary War [1775–82].* Paris, Me., 1825. 36 pp. Reprint ed., New York: Charles P. Everitt, 1940.

767. Sellers, Nathan. Pa. "Extracts from the Diary of Nathan Sellers, [Aug. 1776]." *Pennsylvania Magazine of History and Biography* 16 (1892):191–96.

768. Senter, Isaac. Surgeon. R.I. *The Journal of Isaac Senter, Physician and Surgeon to the Troops Detached from the American Army Encamped at Cambridge, Mass., on a Secret Expedition against Quebec ... September, 1775 [–Jan. 1776].* Philadelphia, 1846. 40 pp. Reprinted in *Magazine of History*, extra no. 42. Reprint ed., New York: Arno Press, 1969. Also in *Proceedings of the Historical Society of Pennsylvania*, vol. 1, no. 5 (1846). Also in Kenneth Roberts, ed., *March to Quebec* (New York: Doubleday, Doran & Co., 1938), pp. 197–241.

769. Sewall, Henry, Jr. Capt. Mass. "General Henry Sewall's Diary, [Mar. 1776–Nov. 1783]." *The Maine Farmer*, 29 June–30 Nov. 1872. Extract in *Historical Magazine*, 2d ser. 10 (1871):128–37.

770. Seymour, William. Sgt. Maj. Del. *A Journal of the Southern Expedition, [Apr.] 1780-[Jan.] 1783.* Wilmington, 1896. 42 pp. Also in *Pennsylvania Magazine of History and Biography* 7 (1883):286–98, 377–94. DLC (Force transcripts), PHi.

771. Shallus, Jacob. Journal, march to Canada, 1776. Manuscript. MH.

772. Shaw, John Robert. G.B. (deserter to Americans). *A Narrative of*

the Life and Travels of John Robert Shaw, the Well-Digger, Now Resident in Lexington, Kentucky. Lexington, 1807. 181 pp. Reprint ed., Louisville: Fowler, 1930.

773. Shaw, Thomas. Me. Diary, 1775-1837. In Windsor Dagget, *A Down-East Yankee from the District of Maine,* pp. 58-61. Portland, Me.: A. J. Huston, 1920. Extract in *Magazine of History,* extra no. 116.

774. Sherburne, Andrew. Seaman. N.H. *Memoirs of Andrew Sherburne: A Pensioner of the Navy of the Revolution.* Utica, N.Y., 1820. 262 pp. 2d ed. Providence, 1831.

775. Shipboard journal, West Indies and Yorktown, 1781-83. Manuscript. NHi.

776. Shreve, John. Lt. N.J. "Personal Narrative of the Services of Lieut. John Shreve of the New Jersey Continental Line [1775-81]." *Magazine of American History* 3, pt. 2 (1879):564-78.

777. Shute, Daniel. Surgeon. Mass. "The Journal of Dr. Daniel Shute, Surgeon in the Revolution, [Aug.] 1781- [Apr.] 1782." *New England Historical and Genealogical Register* 84 (1930):383-89.

778. Shute, Samuel M. Lt. N.J. "Journal of Lieut. Samuel M. Shute [May-Nov. 1779]." In New York (State) Secretary of State, *Journals of the Military Expedition of Major General John Sullivan,* pp. 267- 74. Auburn, 1887. WHi.

779. *Siege of Savannah, in 1779, As Described in Two Contemporaneous Journals of French Officers in the Fleet of Count D'Estaing.* Edited by Charles C. Jones, Jr. Albany, 1874. 70 pp. Reprint ed., New York: Arno Press, 1968.

780. Slade, William. Pvt. [?]. Conn. Prison diary, New York, Nov. 1776-Jan. 1777. In Danske Dandridge, *American Prisoners of the Revolution,* pp. 494-501. Charlottesville: Michie Co., 1911. VtMiS.

781. Slocum, Joshua. Pvt. [?]. Mass. [?]. *An Authentic Narrative of the Life of Joshua Slocum: Containing a Succinct Account of His Revolutionary Services.* Compiled by John Slocum. Hartford, 1883. 105 pp.

782. Smith, Hezekiah. Chaplain. Mass. In Reuben Aldridge Guild, *Chaplain Smith and the Baptists; or, Life, Journals, Letters, and Addresses of the Rev. Hezekiah Smith, D.D., of Haverhill, Massachusetts, 1737-1805.* Philadelphia, 1885. 429 pp. DLC.

783. Smith, James. Col. Pa. *An Account of the Remarkable Occurrences in the Life and Travels of James Smith.* Philadelphia, 1831. [A few pages concern revolutionary war service.]

784. Smith, John. Sgt. R.I. "Sergeant John Smith's Diary of [Sept.-

Dec.] 1776." Edited by Louise Rau. *Mississippi Valley Historical Review* 20 (1933):247-70.

785. Smith, Josiah. Col. N.Y. "Diary of Colonel Josiah Smith from July 23 to September 7, 1776." *Magazine of American History* 17 (1886): 347-48, 437.

786. Smith, Samuel. Pvt. R.I. *Memoirs of the Life of Samuel Smith: Being an Extract from a Journal Written by Himself, from 1776 to 1786.* Middleborough, Mass., 1853. 24 pp. Also in Charles I. Bushnell, ed., *Crumbs for Antiquarians* (New York, 1860), vol. 1, no. 2.

787. Spafford, John. Cpl. N.H. Journal, march to Quebec, Feb.-Apr. 1776. Manuscript. 8 pp. DNA (Pension files).

788. Sproat, James. Chaplain. Conn. "Extracts from the Journal of Rev. James Sproat, Hospital Chaplain of the Middle Department, [Apr.-Oct.] 1778." *Pennsylvania Magazine of History and Biography* 27 (1903):441-45.

789. Sproule, Moses. Pvt. N.J. "A Journal of the Marches Proceedings &c. Compleated by the Army under Command of Major Genl. (John) Sullivan on the Western Expedition ... [May-Oct.] 1779." Edited by R. W. G. Vail. *Quarterly of the New-York Historical Society* 41 (1957): 47-69.

790. Squier, Ephraim. Sgt. Conn. "Diary of Ephraim Squier, Sergeant in the Connecticut Line of the Continental Army [Sept.-Nov. 1775, Sept.-Nov. 1777]." *Magazine of American History* 2, pt. 2 (1878): 685-94. Extract in Kenneth Roberts, ed., *March to Quebec* (New York: Doubleday, Doran & Co. 1938), pp. 619-28. DLC.

791. Stedman, Levi. Pvt. Mass. Orderly book and journal, July 1775-Apr. 1776. Manuscript. 42 pp. DNA (Pension files).

792. Steevens, William. Sgt. Conn. Account book and record book, Jan. 1777-Dec. 1793. Manuscript. 11 pp. DNA (Pension files).

793. Steuben, Friedrich Wilhelm von. Maj. Gen. Prussia. Journal [?], 1778-82. Manuscript. NHi.

794. ———. Journal [?], 1780-81. Manuscript. MH.

795. Stevens, Benjamin. Pvt. Conn. Journal, march to Montreal, Feb.-May 1776. *Daughters of the American Revolution Magazine* 45 (1914):136-40. MBNEH, DLC (Force transcripts).

796. Stevens, Elisha. Conn. *Fragments of Memoranda, Written by Him in the War of the Revolution.* Meriden, Conn., 1922. 22 pp.

797. Stevens, James. Pvt. Mass. "The Revolutionary Journal of James Stevens of Andover, Massachusetts, [Apr. 1775-Apr. 1776]." *Historical Collections of the Essex Institute* 48 (1912): 41-70.

798. Stewart, Jehiel. Pvt. Mass. Journal, New England, Canada, New York, Mar. 1775–Oct. 1779. Manuscript. 134 pp. DNA (Pension files).

799. Stickney, Nathan. Pvt. Mass. Journal, Rhode Island, Aug.-Dec. 1778. Manuscript. 18 pp. DNA (Pension files).

800. Stimson, Jeremy. Surgeon, Mass. "Dr. Stimson's Diary, [Sept.-Oct.] 1776." *Proceedings of the Massachusetts Historical Society* 46 (1912-13):250-52. MHi.

801. Stocking, Abner. Pvt. Conn. *An Interesting Journal of Abner Stocking of Chatham, Connecticut, Detailing the Distressing Events of the Expedition against Quebec . . . [Sept. 1775-Jan. 1776]*. Catskill, N.Y., 1810. Reprinted in *Magazine of History*, extra no. 75. Also in Kenneth Roberts, ed., *March to Quebec* (New York: Doubleday, Doran & Co., 1938), pp. 545-69.

802. Stone, Enos. Capt. Mass. "[Extracts from] Capt. Enos Stone's Journal, [Nov. 1776-Nov. 1777]." *New England Historical and Genealogical Register* 15 (1861):299-304. NRHi.

803. Stone, Josiah. Pvt. Mass. Journal, New England, New York, Dec. 1776-Jan. 1777. Manuscript. 4 pp. DNA (Pension files).

804. Stone, Stephen. Conn. Journal, New York, June 1778-May 1781. In William L. Stone, *The Family of John Stone, One of the First Settlers of Guilford, Conn.*, pp. 30-33. Albany, 1888.

805. Stone, Thomas. Pvt. Waggoner. N.Y. "The Experiences of a Prisoner in the American Revolution, [May 1776-June [?] 1780]." *Journal of American History* 2 (1908):527-29.

806. Storrs, Experience. Lt. Col. Conn. "[Extracts?] from Diary of Lieut. Col. Exp. Storrs, of Mansfield, Cn., [June 1775]." *Proceedings of the Massachusetts Historical Society* 14 (1875-76):84-87. Extracts in *Magazine of American History* 8, pt. 1 (1882):124.

807. Swain, Anthony. Artificer. N.J. Journal, New York City, Mar.-Dec. 1776. Manuscript. 4 pp. DNA (Pension files).

808. Talbot, Silas. Capt. *An Historical Sketch to the End of the Revolutionary War of the Life of Silas Talbot*. New York, 1803. 147 pp. Reprinted as *The Life and Surprising Adventures of Captain Silas Talbot . . . from the Time of His First Going to Sea as a Cabin Boy; Until His Taking Command of the Washington Ship of War* (London, 1806[?]).

809. Tallmadge, Benjamin. Maj. Conn. *Memoir of Col. Benjamin Tallmadge*. New York, 1858. 70 pp. Reprint ed., New York: Arno Press, 1968.

810. Tallmadge, Samuel. Capt. N.Y. "Journal of Samuel Tallmadge, [Dec. 1780–July 1782]." In Almon W. Lauber, ed., *Orderly Books of the Fourth New York Regiment*, pp. 739–85. Albany: University of the State of New York, 1932.

811. Talmadge [Tallmadge?], Samuel. Ens. N.Y. Journal, New York, Sullivan's expedition, Aug. 1778–Sept. 1779. Manuscript. DLC.

812. Teachey, Daniel. Lt. N.C. Journal, 1773–85. Manuscript. 18 pp. DNA (Pension files).

813. Thacher, James. Surgeon. Mass. *A Military Journal during the American Revolutionary War, from 1775–1783.* Boston, 1823. 603 pp. Also, *Military Journal of the American Revolution* (Hartford, Conn., 1862). Reprint ed., New York: Arno Press, 1969.

814. Thayer, Simeon. Capt. R.I. "A Journal of the Indefatigable March of Col. Benedict Arnold ... in the Years 1775–1776." In Edwin Martin Stone, ed., *The Invasion of Canada in 1775*, pp. 1–45. *Collections of the Rhode Island Historical Society*, vol. 6. Providence, 1867. Also in Kenneth Roberts, ed., *March to Quebec* (New York: Doubleday, Doran & Co., 1938), pp. 247–94.

815. Tilden, John Bell. Lt. Pa. "Extracts from the Journal of Lieutenant John Bell Tilden, Second Pennsylvania Line, [Aug.] 1781–[Dec.] 1782." *Pennsylvania Magazine of History and Biography* 19 (1895):51–63, 208–33.

816. Tilghman, Tench. Lt. Col. Md. "Journal of Tench Tilghman [Aug.–Sept. 1775]." In Oswald Tilghman, *Memoir of Lieut. Col. Tench Tilghman*, pp. 79–101. Albany, 1876. Reprint ed., New York: Arno Press, 1971.

817. ———. "Col. Tilghman's Diary of the Siege of Yorktown, [Sept.–Oct. 1781]." In Oswald Tilghman, *Memoir of Lieut. Col. Tench Tilghman*, pp. 103–7. Albany, 1876. Reprint ed., New York: Arno Press, 1971.

818. Todd, Jonathan. Surgeon's mate. Conn. Diary and autobiography, 1756–1819. Manuscript. 22 pp. DNA (Pension files).

819. Tolman, Ebenezer. Pvt. N.H. *See* 846, 867.

820. Topham, John. Capt. R.I. "Journal of the Quebec Expedition, [Oct. 1775–May 1776]." *Magazine of History*, extra no. 50.

821. Town, Zaccheus. Journal, New England, New York, 1776–77. Manuscript. NjR.

822. Trabue, Daniel. Lt. Va. *Colonial Men and Times; Containing the Journal of Col. Daniel Trabue, Some Account of His Ancestry, Life and Travels in Virginia and the Present State of Kentucky during the*

Revolutionary Period. Edited by Lillie Du Puy Van Culin Harper. Philadelphia: Innes & Sons, 1916. 624 pp.

823. Treat, Robert. Cpl. Conn. Journal, Saratoga campaign, Aug.-Oct. 1777. Manuscript. 22 pp. DNA (Pension files).

824. Tremper, Lawrence. Lt. N.Y. Journal, northern New York, Mar. 1783-Nov. 1784. Manuscript. DLC.

825. Trevett, John. Capt. R.I. "Diary of John Trevett, Captain of Marines, [*Nov.* 1775-May 1782?]." In Charles R. Smith, *Marines in the Revolution*, pp. 325-42. Washington, D.C.: Government Printing Office, 1975. Also in *Rhode Island Historical Magazine* 6 (1885-86): 72-74, 106-10, 194-99, 271-78; 7 (1886-87):38-45, 151-60, 205-8. RNHi.

826. Trumbull, Benjamin. Chaplain. Conn. "A Concise Journal of Minutes of the Principal Movements towards St. John's of the Siege and Surrender of the Forts There in 1775, [July-Nov. 1775]." *Collections of the Connecticut Historical Society* 7 (1899):137-73. CtHi.

827. ———. "Journal of the Campaign at New York, [July 1776-Feb. 1777]." *Collections of the Connecticut Historical Society* 7 (1899): 175-218. CtHi.

828. Trumbull, John. Lt. Col. Conn. *Autobiography, Reminiscences and Letters of John Trumbull from 1756-1841.* New York, London, New Haven, 1841. 439 pp.

829. Trumbull, Jonathan. Lt. Col. Conn. "Minutes of Occurrences Respecting the Siege and Capture of York in Virginia, Extracted from the Journal of Jonathan Trumbull, Secretary to the General, [Aug.-Nov.] 1781." *Proceedings of the Massachusetts Historical Society* 14 (1875-76):331-38.

830. Tucker, Daniel. Privateer, capt. Me. "Capt. Daniel Tucker in the Revolution: An Autobiographical Sketch, [1775-88] ." *Collections and Proceedings of the Maine Historical Society*, 2d ser. 8 (1897):225-54.

831. Turner, Jacob. N. C. Diary, 1778. Manuscript. Nc-Ar. [From the brief description in Matthews, *Manuscript American Diaries* (entry 702) this appears to be an orderly book rather than a diary.]

832. Tuttle, Timothy. Sgt. N.J. Journal, 1775-76. Manuscript. NjHi.

833. Twiss, Jonathan. Drummer. Conn. Journal, 1778. Manuscript. Ct (copy).

834. Vail, Christopher. Pvt. and privateer. N.Y. Journal of service in Connecticut militia, on board a privateer and as a prisoner of war, July 1775-Aug. 1782. Manuscript. MH (Sparks manuscripts), DLC (Force transcripts).

835. Vance, David. Capt. N.C. Memoir of battle of King's Mountain. *American Monthly Magazine* 17 (1900): 508-17.

836. Van Cortlandt, Philip. Brig. Gen. N.Y. "Autobiography of Philip Van Cortlandt, Brigadier-General in the Continental Army, [1775-83]." *Magazine of American History* 2, pt. 1 (1878):278-98.

837. Vanderslice, Henry. Wagonmaster. Pa. Journal, Mar. 1777-June 1778. In Howard Vanderslice and Howard Norman Monnett, *Van der Slice and Allied Families*, pp. 140-61. Los Angeles: Neuner Corp., 1931.

838. Van Dyke, John. Capt. N.Y. "Narrative of Confinement in the *Jersey* Prison Ship, by John Van Dyke, Captain in Lamb's Regiment, N.Y.S.A., [1779]." *Historical Magazine* 7 (1863): 147-51.

839. Van Hovenburgh, Rudolphus. Lt. N.Y. "Journal of Lieut. Rudolphus Van Hovenburgh, [June-Dec. 1779]." In New York (State) Secretary of State, *Journals of the Military Expedition of Major General John Sullivan*, pp. 275-84. Auburn, 1887.

840. Vose, Joseph. Lt. Col. "Journal of Lieutenant-Colonel Joseph Vose, April-July, 1776." Edited by Henry Winchester Cunningham. *Publications of the Colonial Society of Massachusetts* 7 (1900-1902): 248-62. Reprint ed., Cambridge, Mass., 1905.

841. Wadsworth, Peleg. Gen. *A Story about a Little Good Boy; How He Became a Great Man and Had Little Good Boys of His Own.* Portland, Me.: privately printed, 1903. 49 pp.

842. Waldo, Albigence. Surgeon. Conn. "Diary Kept at Valley Forge by Albigence Waldo, Surgeon in the Continental Army, [Nov.] 1777-[Jan.] 1778." *Historical Magazine* 5 (1861):129-34, 169-72. Also in *Pennsylvania Magazine of History and Biography* 21 (1897):299-323. Also in *Annals of Medical History* 10 (1928):486-97. Also, separately published, New York: Paul B. Hoeber, 1928.

843. Walker, Abel. Col. N.H. Journal, march to Quebec, Feb. 1776. In Henry H. Saunderson, *History of Charleston, N.H., the Old No. 4 Embracing the Part Born by Its Inhabitants in the Indian, French and Revolutionary Wars*, p. 585. Claremont, N.H., 1876.

844. Walker, Felix. N.C. *Memoirs of the Late the Hon. Felix Walker of North Carolina . . . from His Original Manuscript of Autobiography.* Edited by Samuel R. Walker. New Orleans, 1877. 19 pp.

845. Walters, Michael. Pa. Journal and travel log, Sandusky expedition, May-Oct. 1782. *Western Reserve Historical Society Tract*, no. 89 (1899), pp. 177-88.

846. Ware, Joseph. Sgt. Mass. "A Journal of a March from Cambridge

on an Expedition against Quebec, in Col. Benedict Arnold's Detachment, Sept. 13, 1775 [-Sept. 1776?]." *New England Historical and Genealogical Register* 6 (1852):129-45. DLC (Force transcripts). [Cf. Wild, Ebenezer, and Tolman, Ebenezer. For contested authorship of this journal see Justin H. Smith, *Arnold's March from Cambridge to Quebec* (New York: G.P. Putnam, 1938), pp. 43-48; and Kenneth Roberts, ed., *March to Quebec* (New York: Doubleday, Doran & Co., 1938), pp. xii-xiii.]

847. Warren, Benjamin. Capt. Mass. "Extracts from Benjamin Warren's Diary, Saratoga, [July-Oct.] 1777; Cherry Valley, [July-Nov.] 1778." *Journal of American History* 3 (1909):201-16, 377-84. MH (Sparks manuscripts).

848. Warren, John. Surgeon. Mass. Journal, Apr. 1775-May 1776. In John C. Warren, *Genealogy of Warren, with Some Historical Sketches,* pp. 85-98. Boston, 1854.

849. Washington, George. Commander-in-Chief. Va. *The Diaries of George Washington, 1748-99.* Edited by John C. Fitzpatrick. Boston and New York: Houghton, Mifflin, 1925. 4 vols. Also, *The Diaries of George Washington,* edited by Donald Jackson and Dorothy Twohig (Charlottesville: University of Virginia Press, 1976-).

850. Watson, Elkanah. Pvt. R.I. *Men and Times of the Revolution; or, Memoirs of Elkanah Watson, Including Journals of Travels in Europe and America, from 1777 to 1842, with His Correspondence with Public Men and Reminiscences and Incidents of the Revolution.* Edited by Winslow C. Watson. New York, 1856. 560 pp. [A few pages concern military service in 1775].

851. Weare, Nathan. Lt. N.H. Journal, Apr.-June 1777. In Warren Brown, *History of the Town of Hampton Falls, New Hampshire, from the Time of the First Settlement,* pp. 244-49. Manchester, N.H.: J. B. Clarke, 1900.

852. Webb, Nathaniel. Sgt. Maj. N.Y. "Journal of Sergeant Nathaniel Webb, [June-Aug. 1779]." In New York (State) Secretary of State, *Journals of the Military Expedition of Major General John Sullivan,* pp. 285-87. Auburn, 1887. NElmHi.

853. ———. "Continuation of Nathaniel Webb's Journal, [Sept.-Oct. 1779]." *Proceedings of the New York State Historical Association* 6 (1906):87-93.

854. Webb, Samuel Blachley. Col. Conn. *Correspondence and Journals of Samuel Blachley Webb.* Edited by Worthington Chauncey Ford. 3 vols. New York, 1893-94. Reprint ed., New York: Arno Press, 1969.

855. Wells, Bayze. Sgt. Conn. "Journal of Bayze Wells, of Farmington; May 1775–February 1777, at the Northward and in Canada." *Collections of the Connecticut Historical Society* 7 (1899):239-96.

856. Weston, Abner. Cpl. Mass. Journals, Rhode Island, New York, July–Oct. 1780, Sept.–Dec. 1781. Manuscript. 70 pp. DNA (Pension files).

857. Wheeler, Bennett. Maj. R.I. "Extract from the Diary of Major Bennett Wheeler: The British in Rhode Island." *Publications of the Rhode Island Historical Society*, n.s. 6 (1898):91.

858. Wheeler, Rufus. Lt. Mass. "Journal of Lieut. Rufus Wheeler of Rowley; Fort Ticonderoga, July 23 to December 10, 1776." *Historical Collections of the Essex Institute* 68 (1932):371-77. MSaE.

859. Whipple, Jabez. Lt. R.I. Journal, Rhode Island, Sept.–Oct. 1777. Manuscript. 4 pp. DNA (Pension files).

860. Whitcombe, Benjamin. Lt. N.H. "A Journal of a Scout from Crown Point, to St. John's Chamblee &c. &c. by Lieut. Benjamin Whitcombe and Four Men [July, 1776]." *American Historical Record* 1 (1872):437-38.

861. White, Ammi. Artificer. Mass. Journal, constructing fortifications at New York City, Apr. 1776–Jan. 1777. Manuscript. 33 pp. DNA (Pension files).

862. White, E. Journal, 1780. Manuscript. MBAt.

863. White, John. Privateer, capt. Mass. Journal interleaved in almanacs, 1774-76, 1778, 1787-90. Manuscript. DLC.

864. White, Joseph. Sgt. Mass. *An Narrative of Events, As They Occurred from Time to Time, in the Revolutionary War; with an Account of the Battles of Trenton, Trenton-Bridge, and Princeton.* Charlestown, Mass., 1833. 30 pp.

865. Widger, William. Privateer. Mass. "Diary of William Widger, Kept at Mill Prison, England, [Jan.-Dec.] 1781." *Historical Collections of the Essex Institute* 73 (1937):311-47; 74 (1938):22-48, 142-58.

866. Wigglesworth, Edward. Col. Mass. Extracts from journal, upstate New York, Oct.–Nov. 1776. In Euphemia Vale Smith, *History of Newburyport; from the Earliest Settlement of the Country to the Present Time*, pp. 357-59. Newburyport, Mass., 1854.

867. Wild, Ebenezer. Cpl. Mass. "A Journal of a March from Cambridge, on an Expedition against Quebec in Colonel Benedict Arnold's Detachment, Sept. 13, 1775 [-June 1776]." *Proceedings of the Massachusetts Historical Society*, 2d ser. 2 (1885-86):267-75.

[Cf. Ware, Joseph, and Tolman, Ebenezer. For contested authorship of this journal see Justin H. Smith, *Arnold's March from Cambridge to Quebec* (New York: G. P. Putnam, 1938), pp. 43–48; and Kenneth Roberts, ed., *March to Quebec* (New York: Doubleday, Doran & Co., 1938), pp. xii–xiii.]

868. ———. "The Journal of Ebenezer Wild (1776–1781), Who Served as Corporal, Sergeant, Ensign, and Lieutenant in the American Army of the Revolution." *Proceedings of the Massachusetts Historical Society*, 2d ser. 6 (1890–91):78–160.

869. Wilder, Joseph. Sgt. Mass. Journal, Rhode Island, July–Dec. 1777. 12 pp. DNA (Pension files).

870. Wilkinson, James. Brig. Gen. Md. *Memoirs of My Own Times*. 3 vols. Philadelphia, 1816.

871. Willett, Marinus. Col. N.Y. *A Narrative of the Military Actions of Colonel Marinus Willett, taken Chiefly from His Own Manuscript*. Edited by William M. Willett. New York, 1831. 162 pp. Reprint ed., New York: Arno Press, 1969.

872. Williams, Ennion. Maj. Pa. "Journal of Major Ennion Williams on His Journey to the American Camp at Cambridge in New England, [Oct.] 1775." *Pennsylvania Archives*, 2d ser. 15:7–20.

873. Woodbridge, Theodore. Maj. Conn. Journal, 1780–83. Manuscript. DLC.

874. Woodruff, Oliver. Pvt. Conn. Memoir. *Daughters of the American Revolution Magazine* 44 (1914):260–63.

875. Wright, Aaron. Pvt. Pa. "Revolutionary Journal of Aaron Wright, [June] 1775 [–Mar. 1776]." *Historical Magazine* 6 (1862): 208–12.

876. Young, William. Sgt. Pa. "Journal of Sergeant William Young, Written during the Jersey Campaign in the Winter of 1776–7." *Pennsylvania Magazine of History and Biography* 8 (1884):255–78. PHi.

MAJOR-SUBJECT INDEX

☆

As with other topical bibliographies, a full exploitation of this Guide can be gained only by reading the entries. This "index" offers a quick reference to approximately fifty major subjects. A few subjects, most notably "Army," are not included because they appear so frequently as to render an index impractical. Page numbers are italicized; all other references are to the numbered entries.

Alabama, 45, 184, 209, 216

Blacks, 191, 192, 212, 245, 247

Cincinnati, Society of the, 22, 56, 64, 74, 111, 129, 185, 222, 229

Connecticut, ix, 3, 6, 7, 72, 73, 87, 88, 146, 159, 182, 186, 224, 225, 230, 245, 58, 60, 338-876 passim

Delaware, 8, 56, 321, 347, 349, 629, 755, 770

District of Columbia, 121

France, 51, 67, 74, 112, 128, 129, 166, 170, 197, 231, 331, 338-876 passim

Georgia, 10, 11, 13, 27, 89, 165, 175, 211, 322, 508

Illinois, x, 79, 156, 157, 242

Indiana, x, 90, 122, 243, 244

Indians, 163, 220

Irish Americans, 77, 123, 180, 190, 198, 199

Jews, 248

Kentucky, 62, 207, 229, 450

Maine, 65, 66, 91, 92, 126, 139, 152, 163, 188, 226, 241, 276, 328, 341, 383, 400, 509, 558, 743, 773, 830

Marines, 62, 142, 172, 176, 207, 218, 337, 566, 603,

Maryland, 14, 121, 178, 193, 232, 277, 319, 376, 665, 816, 817, 870,

Massachusetts, x, 3, 23, 22, 46, 53, 71, 93, 113, 126, 130, 154, 155, 181, 208, 214, 220, 222, 227, 239, 247, 250, 60, 312, 315, 338-876 passim

Militia, 2, 8, 71, 115, 165, 174, 179, 224, 236, 240, 407, 575

Mississippi, 94, 164

Missouri, x, 153, 177

Navy, 5, 1, 2, 4, 35, 37, 47, 63, 72, 142, 143, 161, 165, 172, 180, 186, 202, 207, 224, 233, 240, 273, 334, 335, 500, 524, 553, 581, 675, 710, 775, 808

New England, 329

New Hampshire, 3, 12, 53, 95, 114, 132, 133, 141, 162, 171, 204, 219, 238, 314, 338-876 passim

New Jersey, x, 6, 64, 234, 235, 236, 310, 338-876 passim

New York, 16, 17, 18, 55, 69, 96,